This book belongs to

. . . .

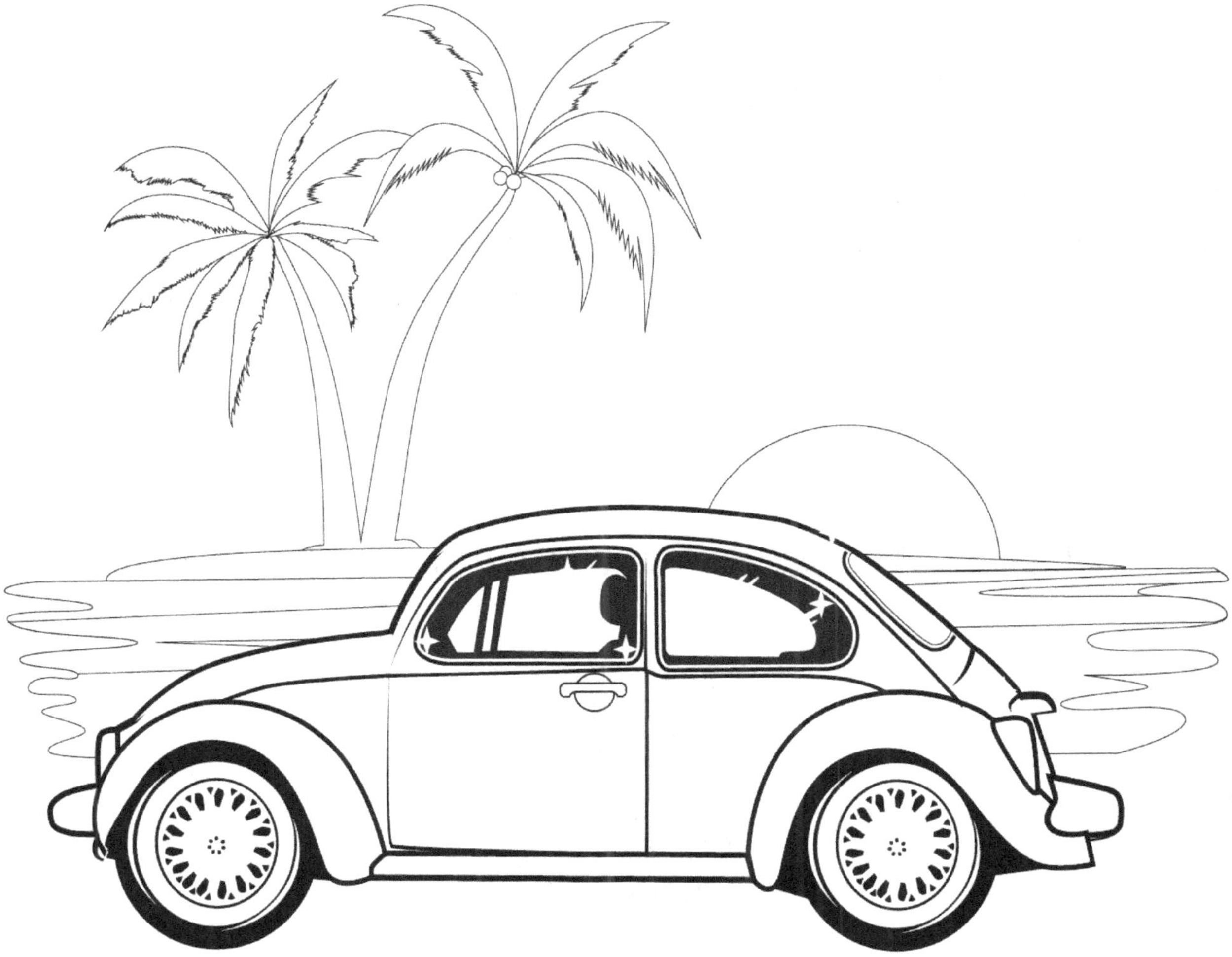

Copyright © 2020 by Blue blend

Blue blend

Design by Blue blend

All rights reserved. No part of this book may be reproduced without written permission of the copyright owner, except for the use of limited quotations for the purpose of book reviews.

Follow us

https://www.amazon.com/author/blueblend

Test Your Colors Here

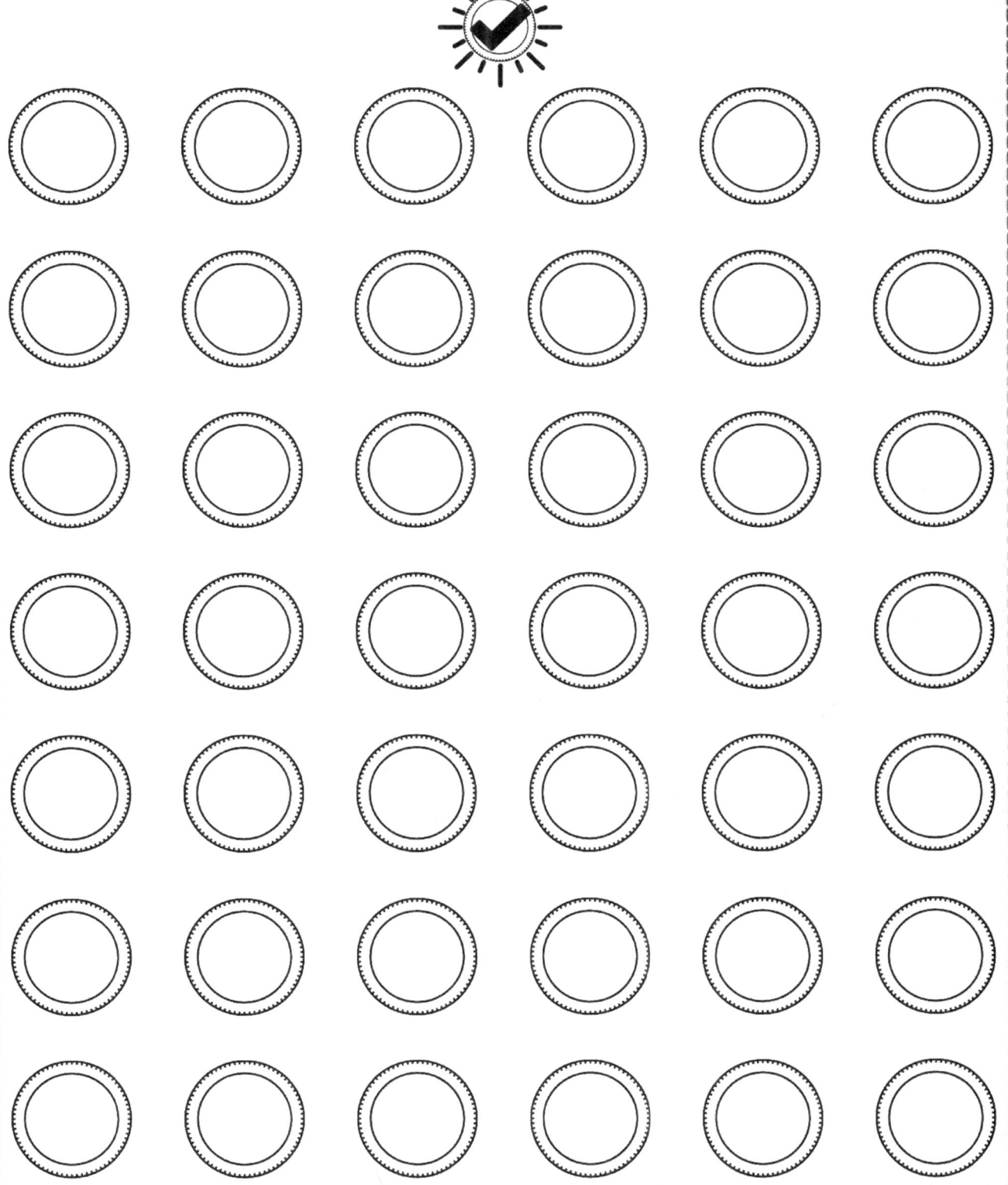

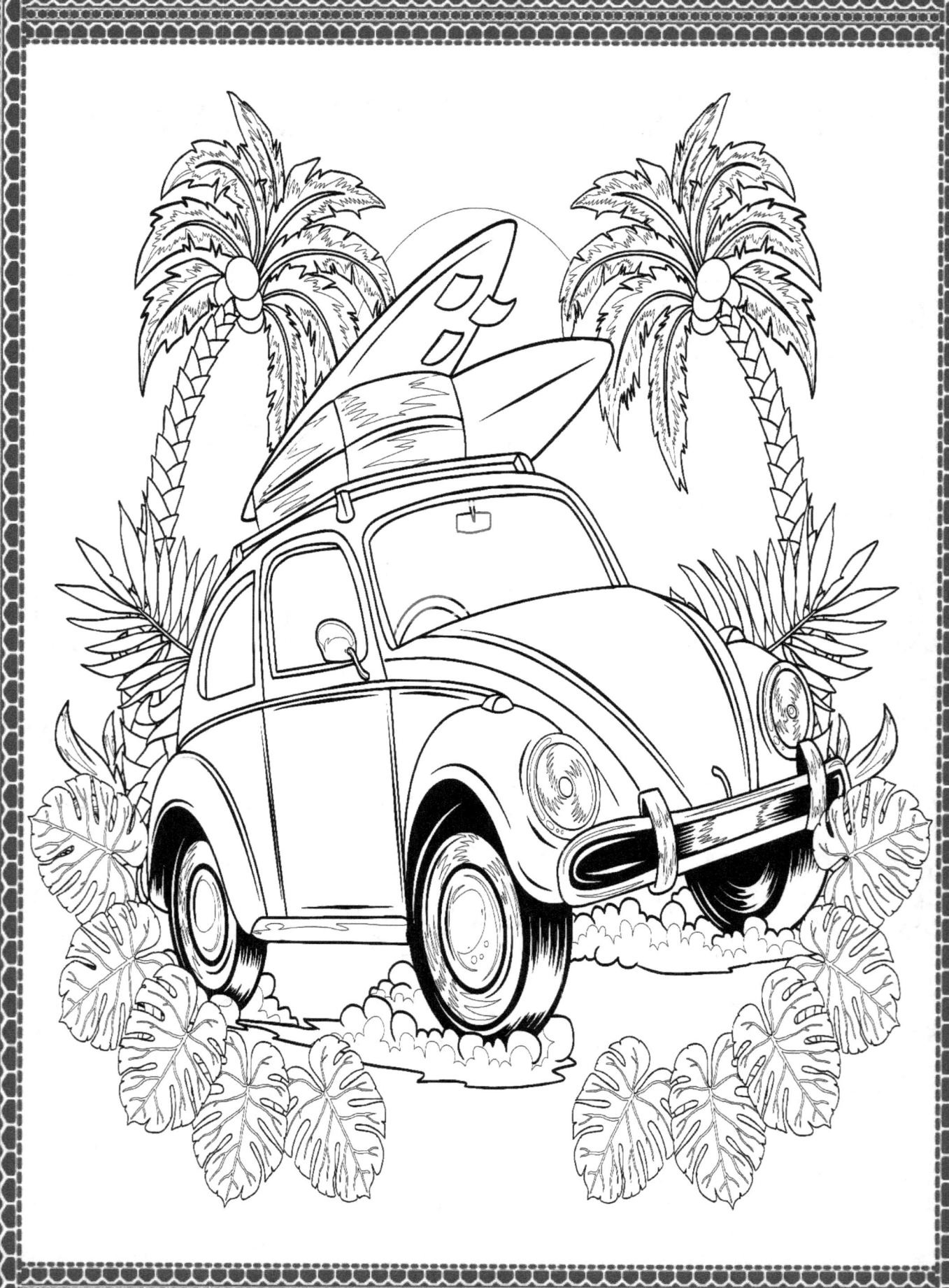

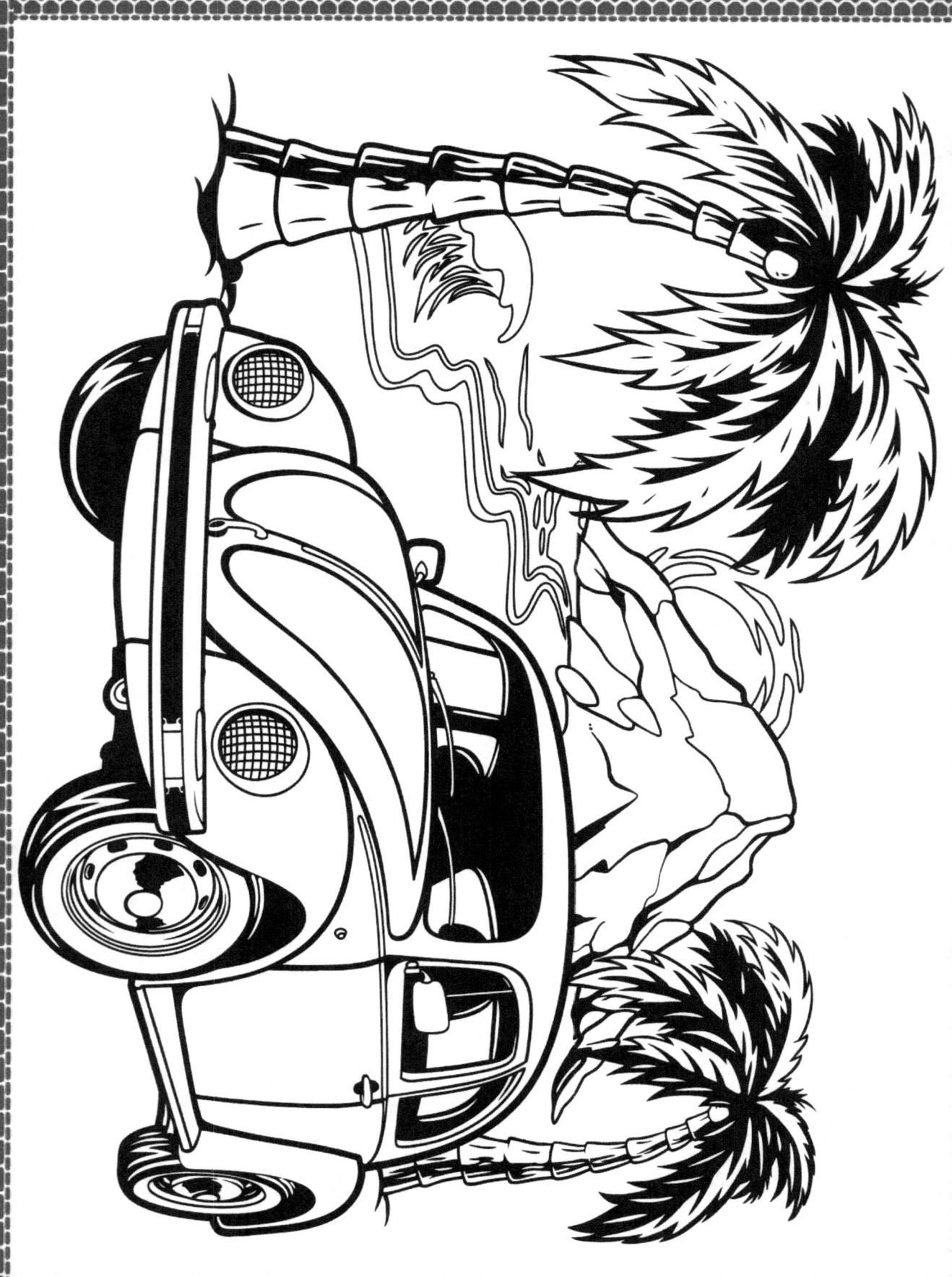

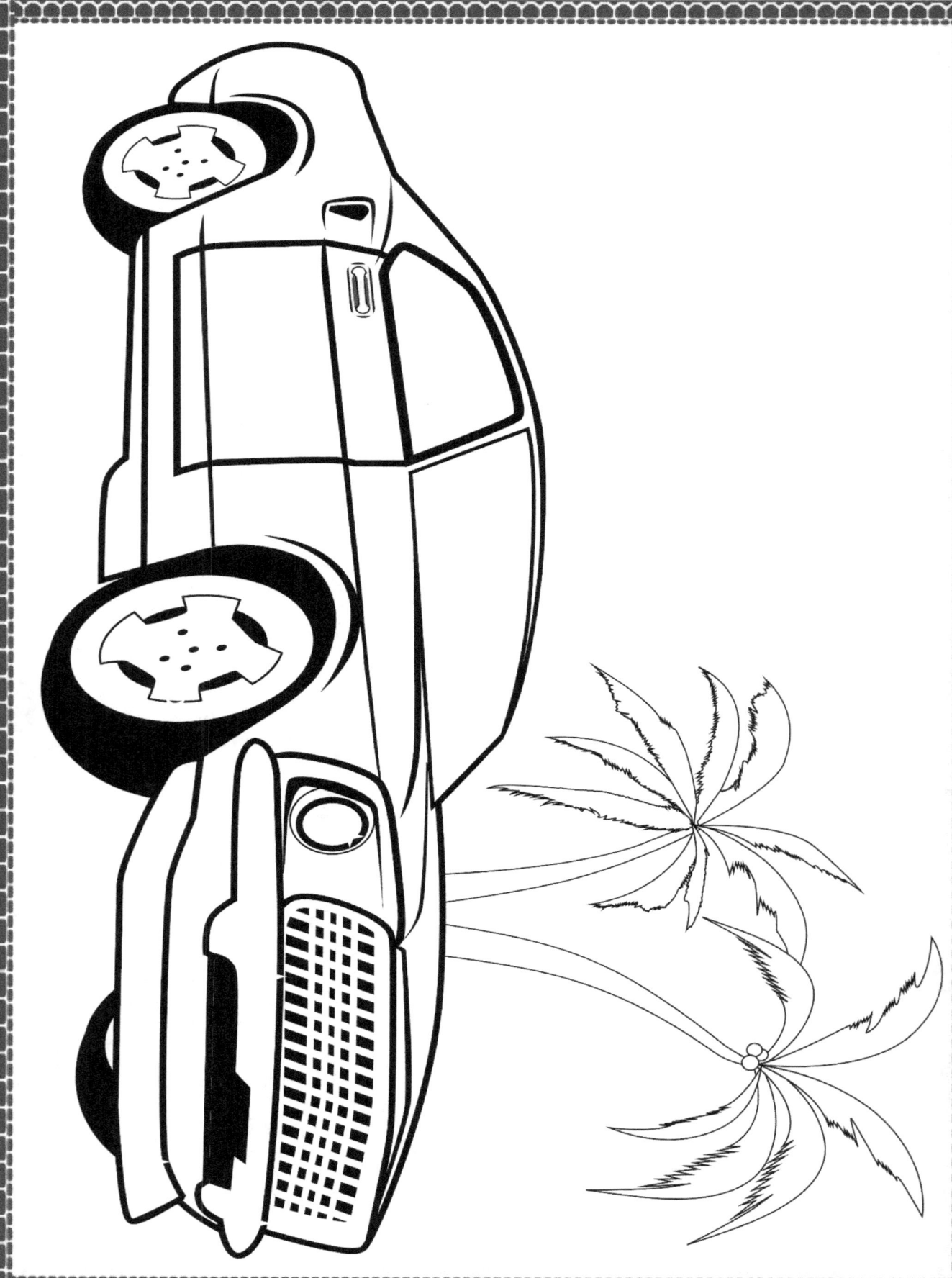

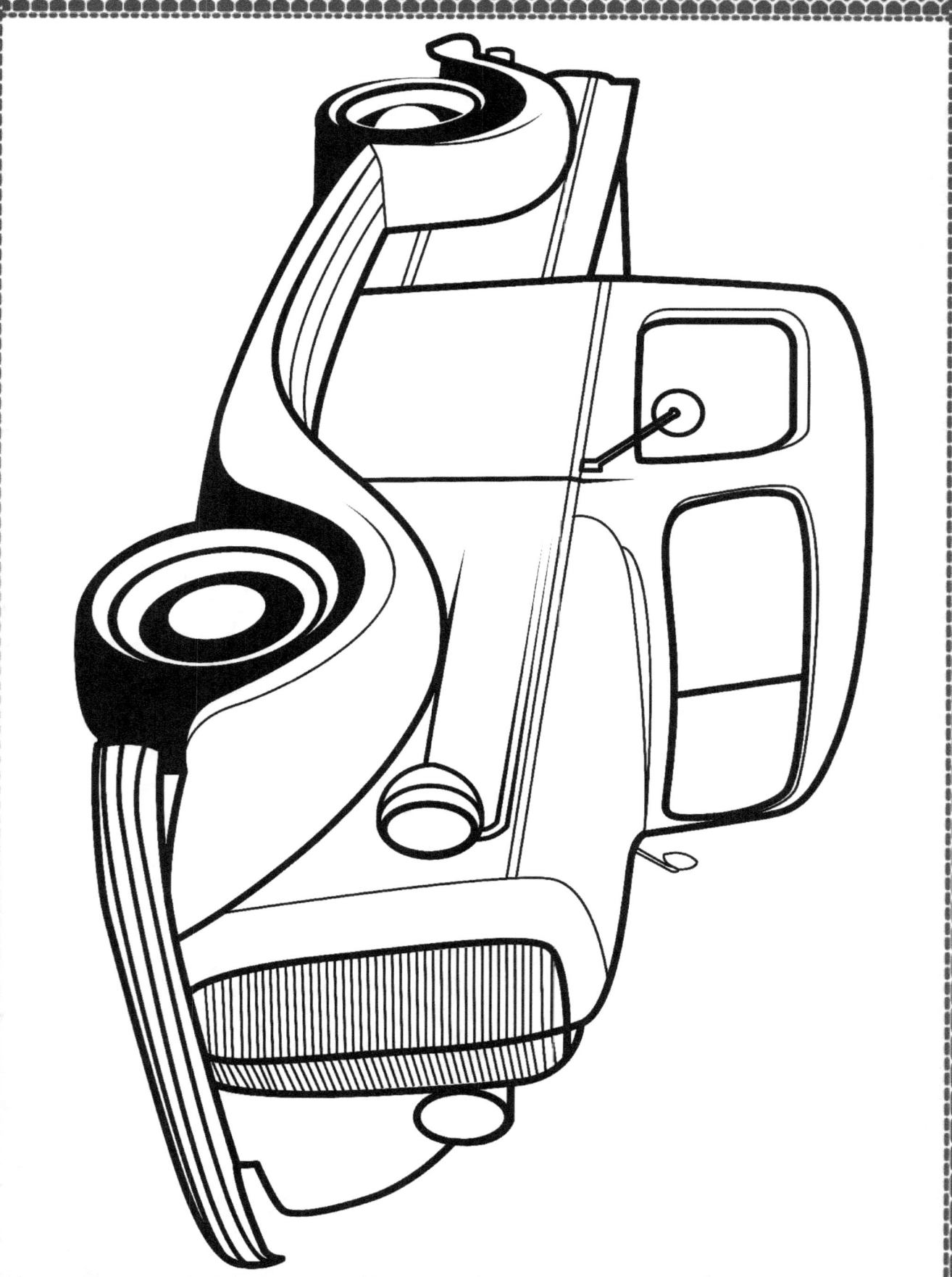

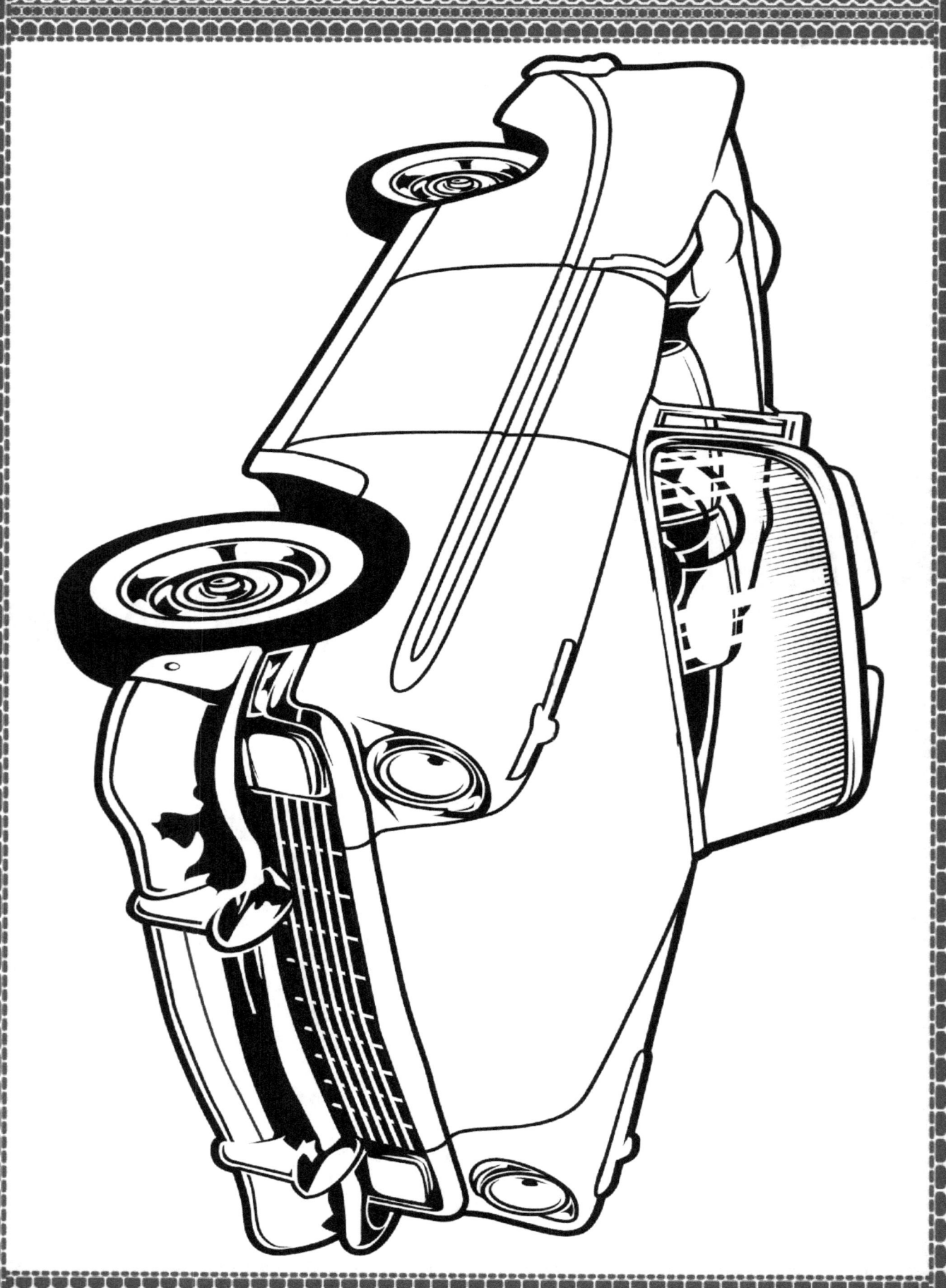

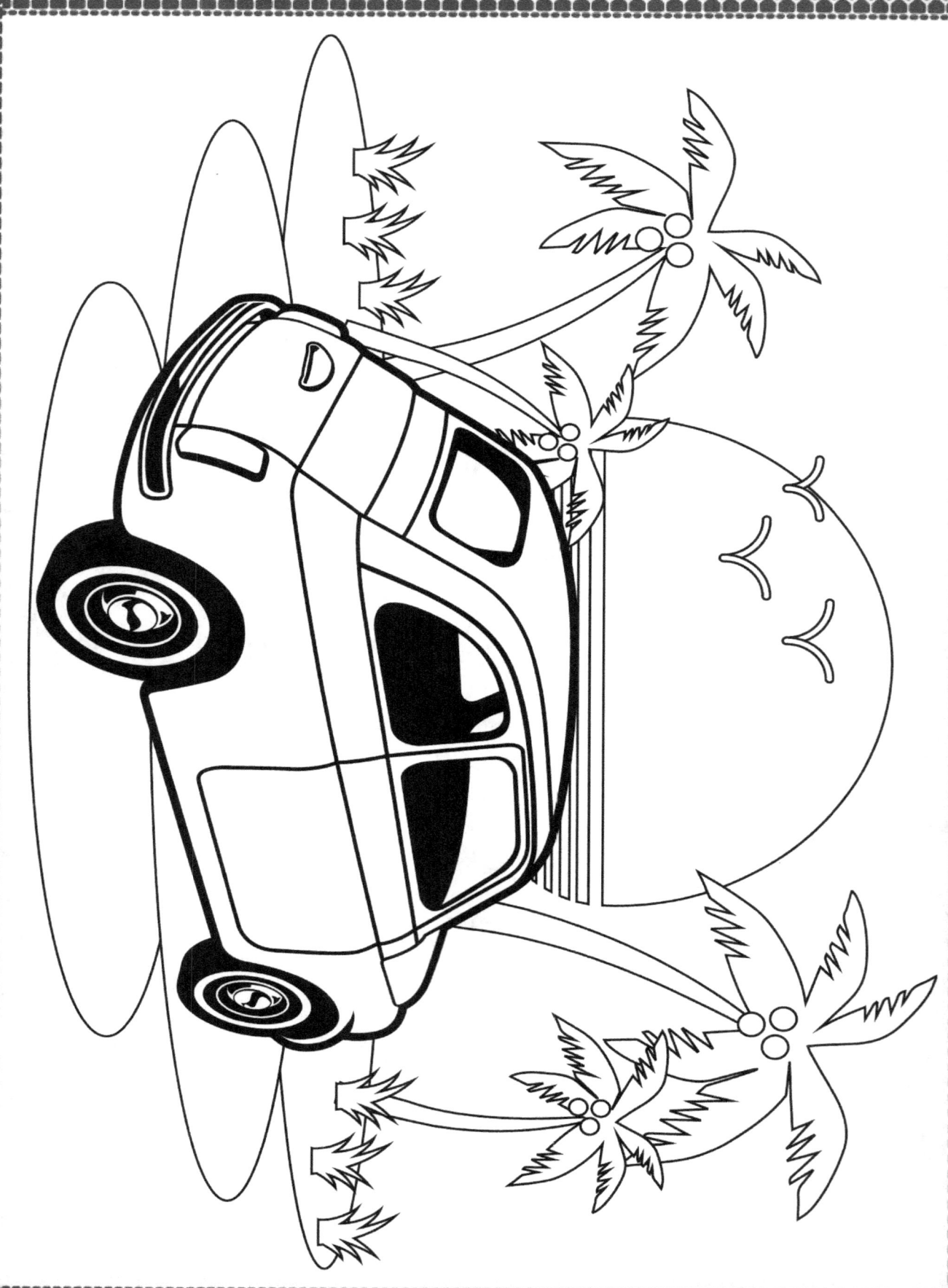

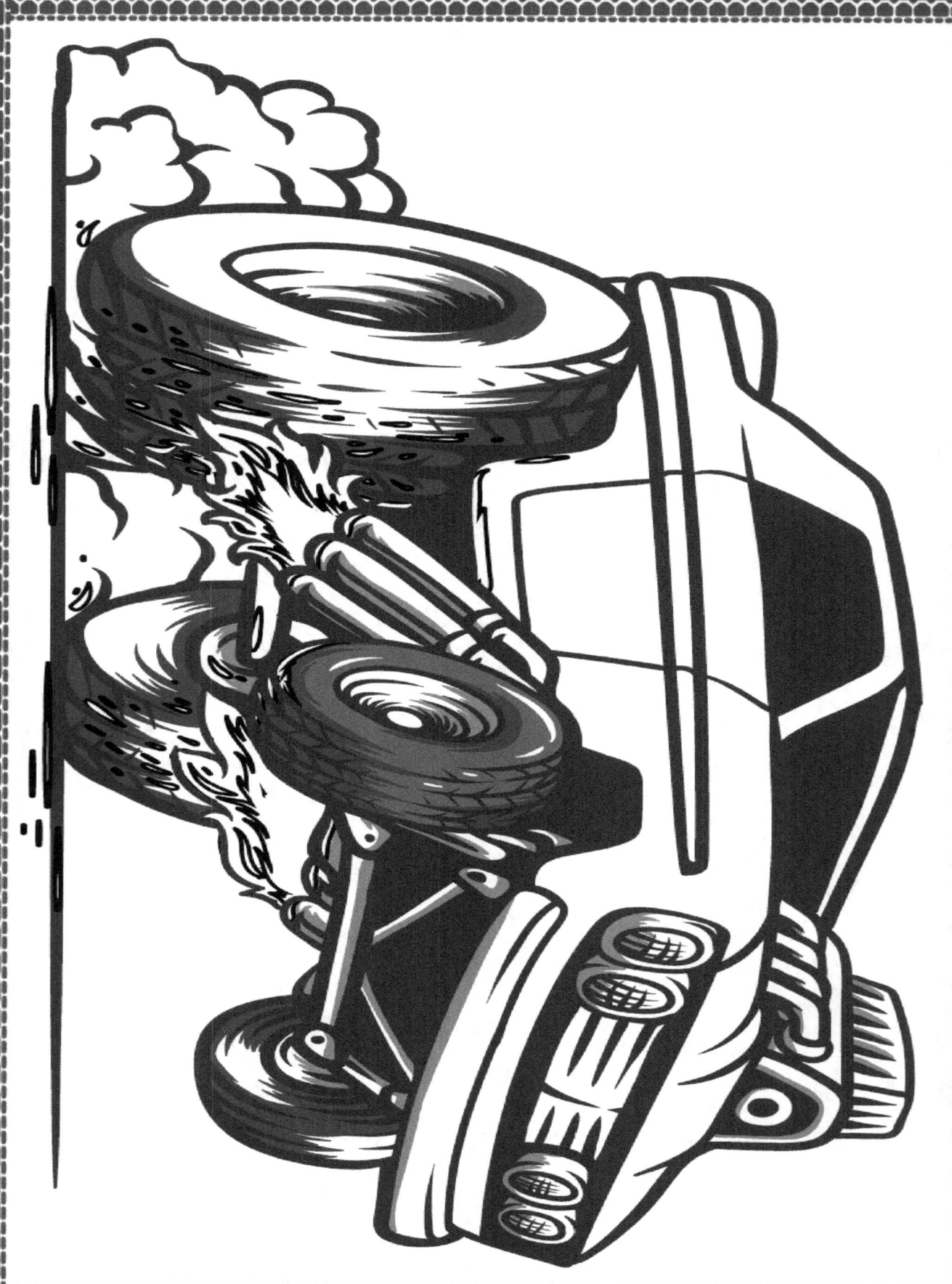

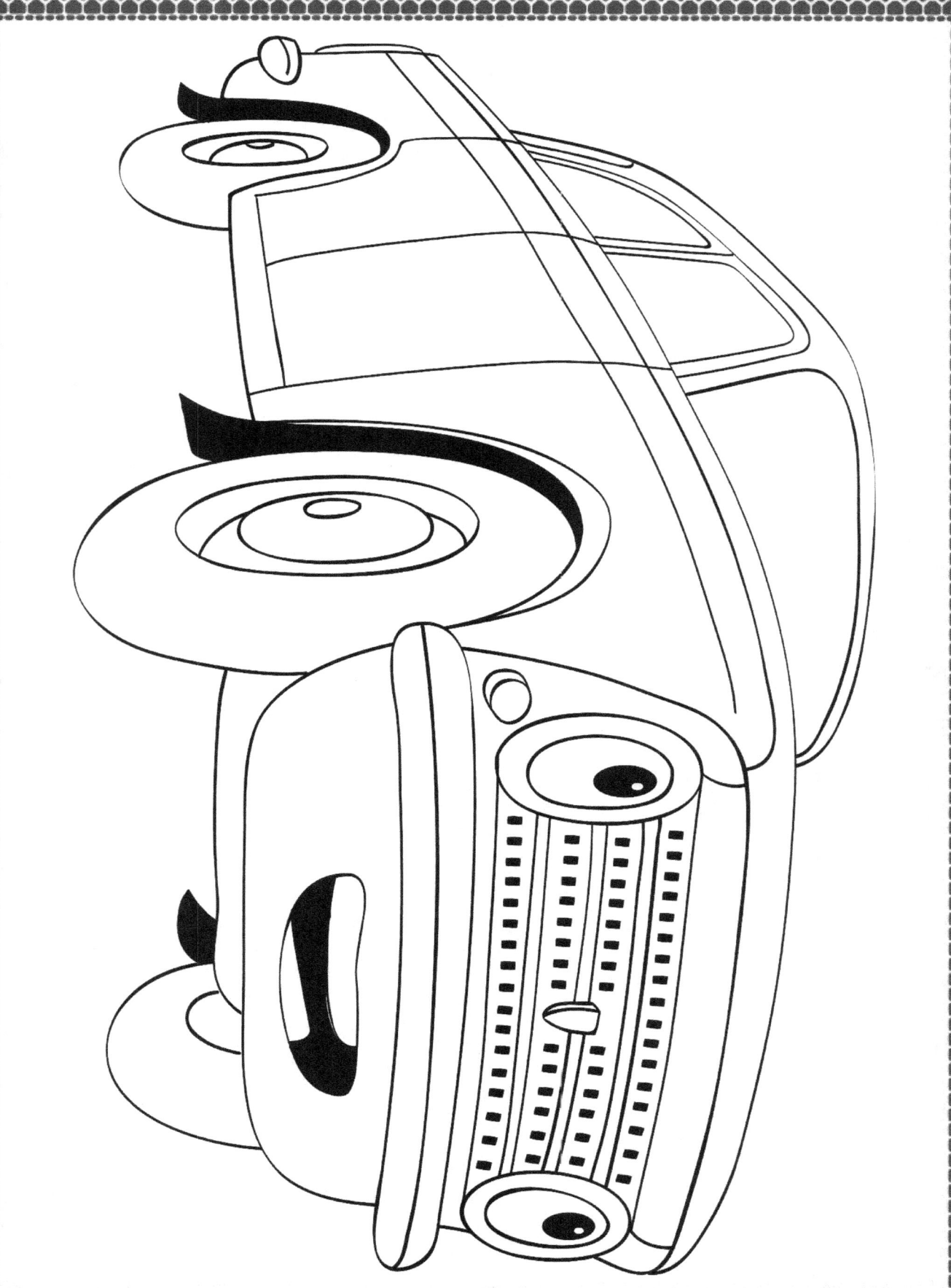

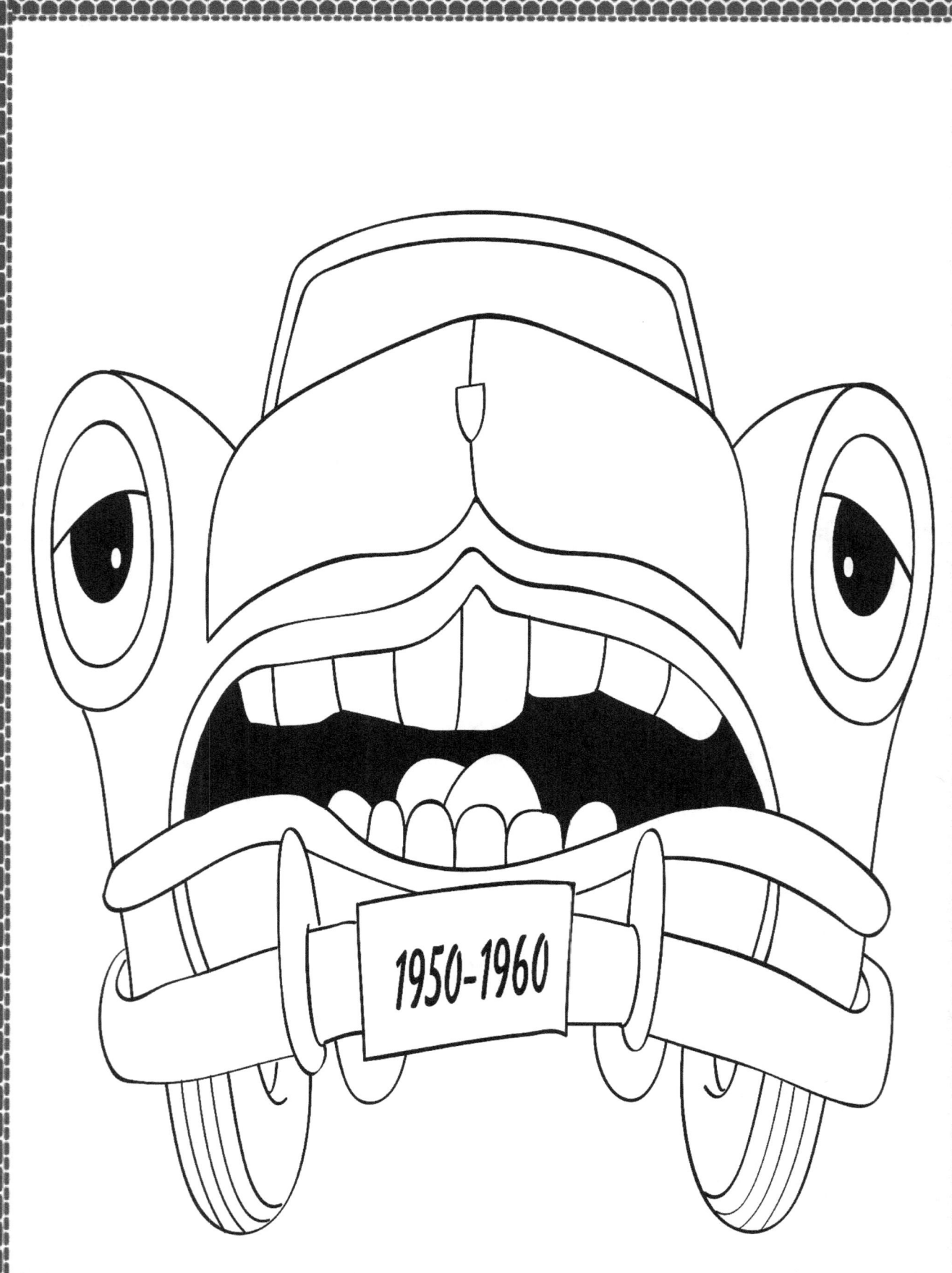

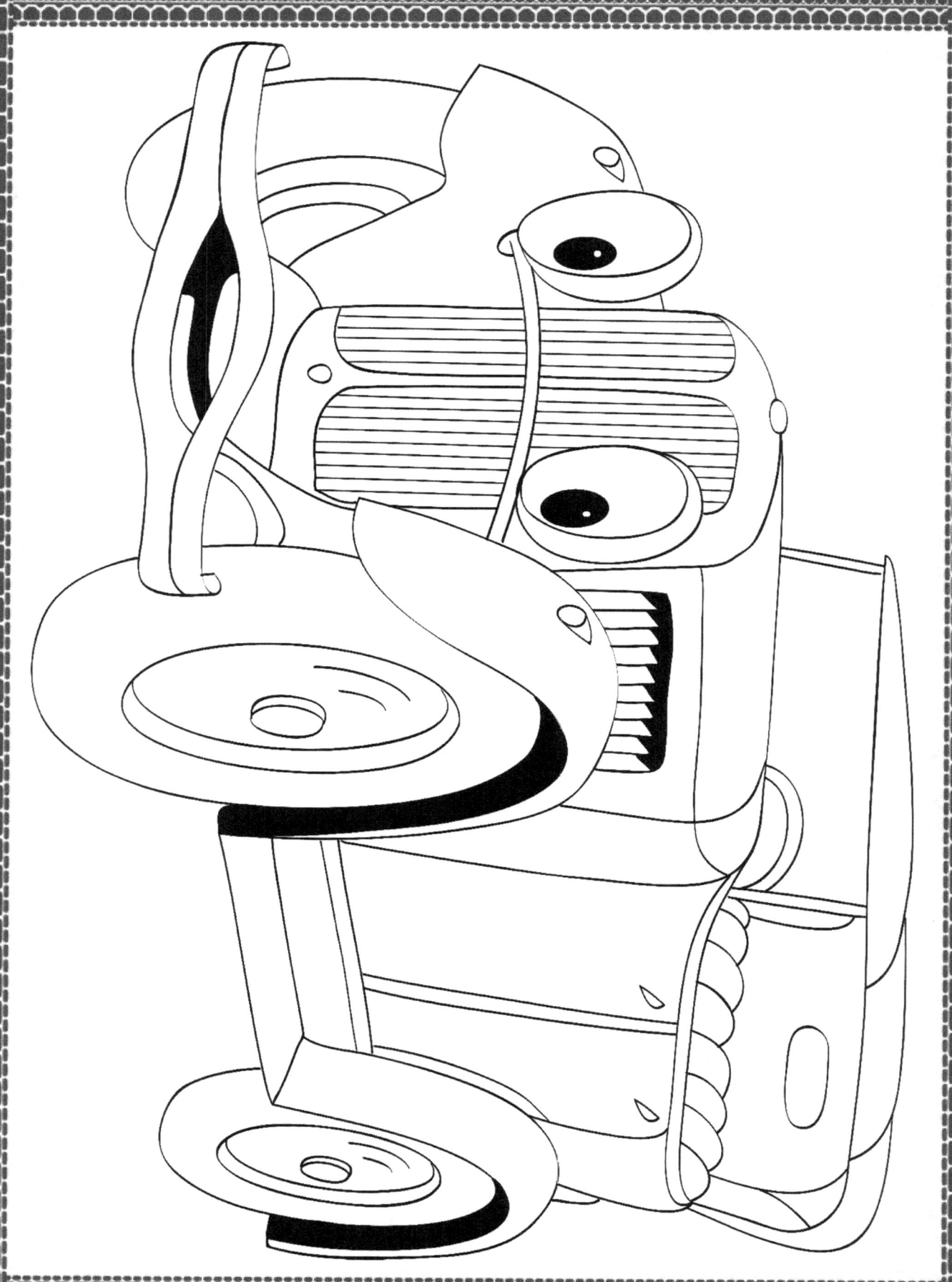

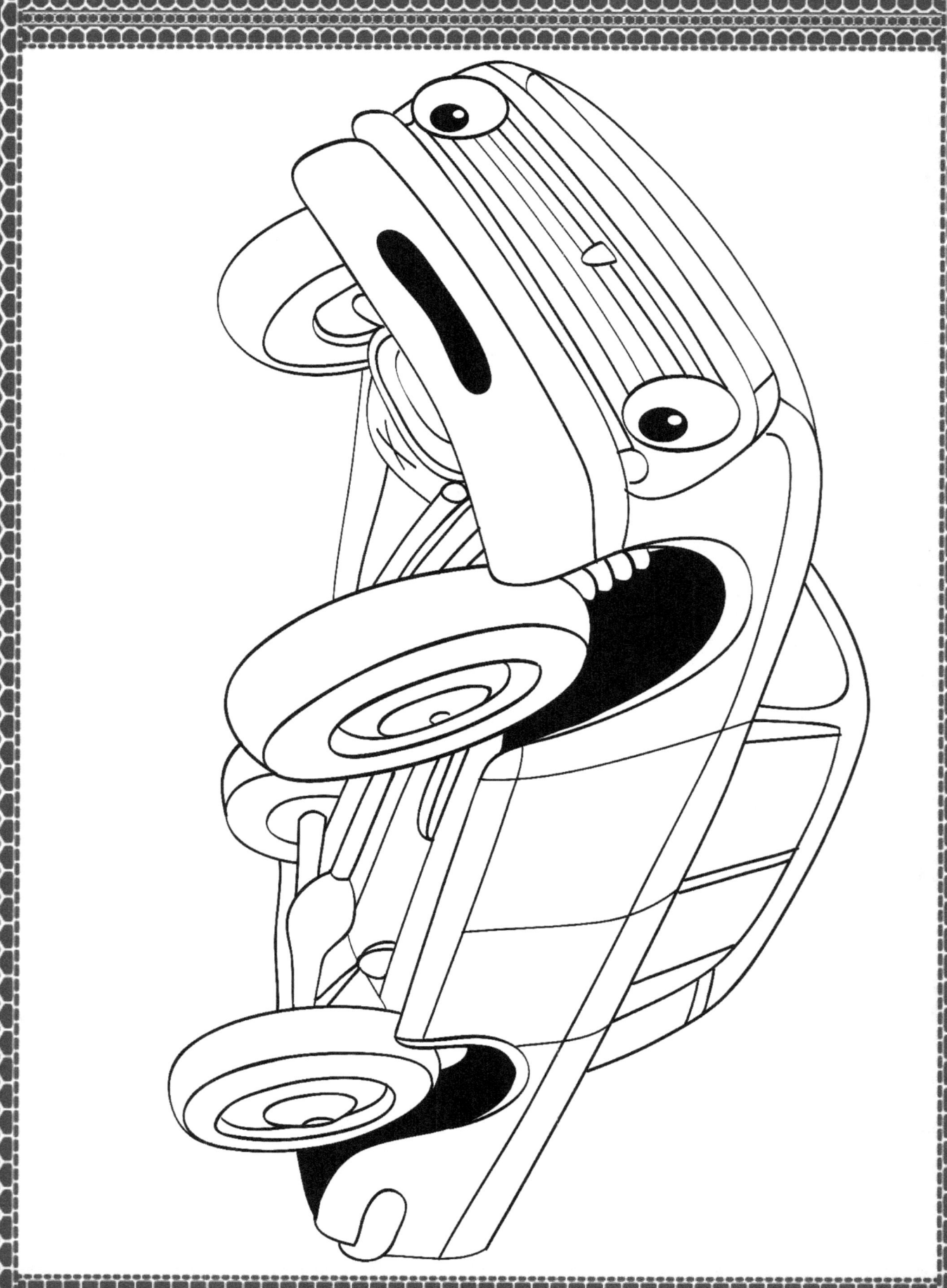

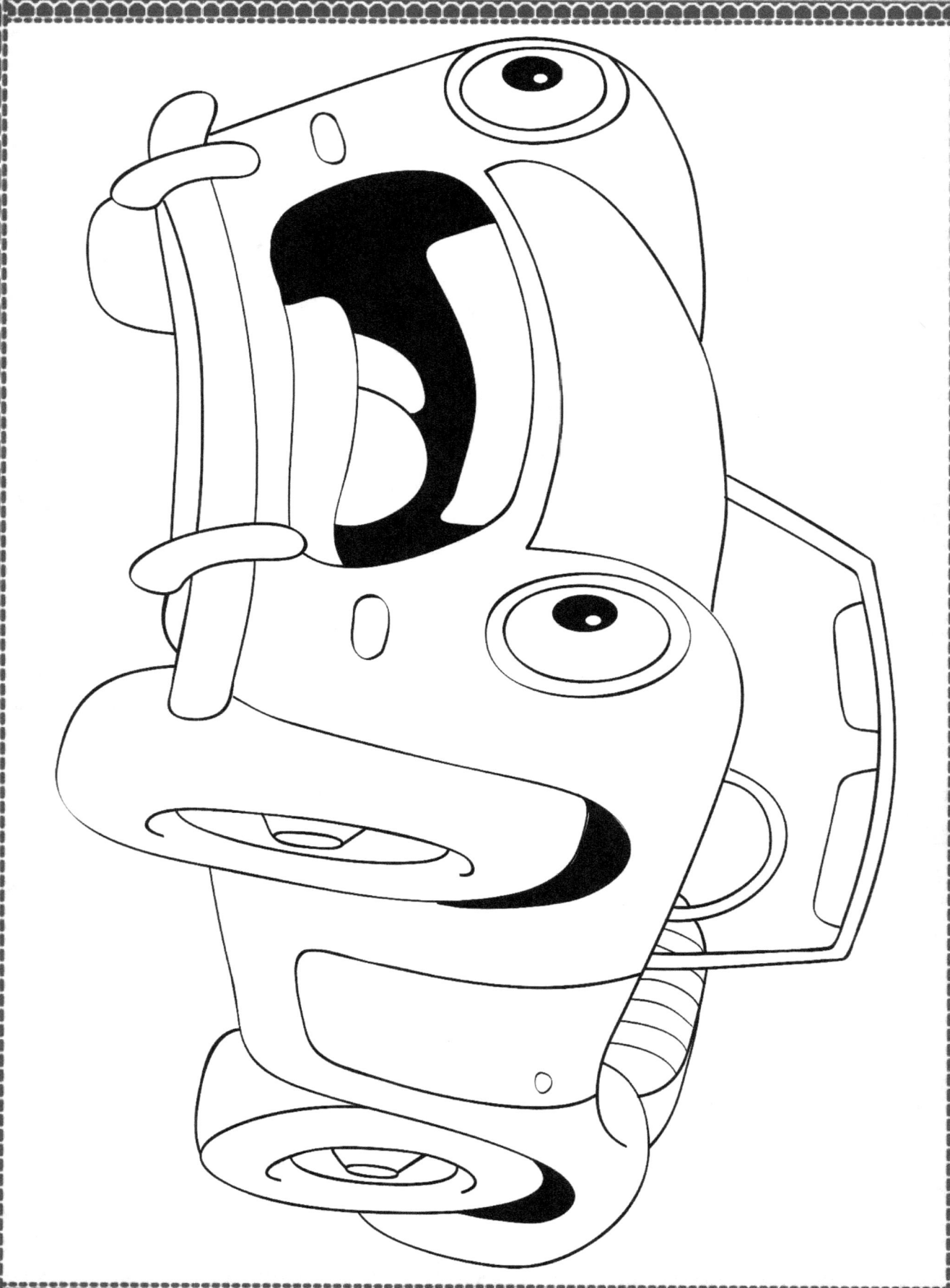

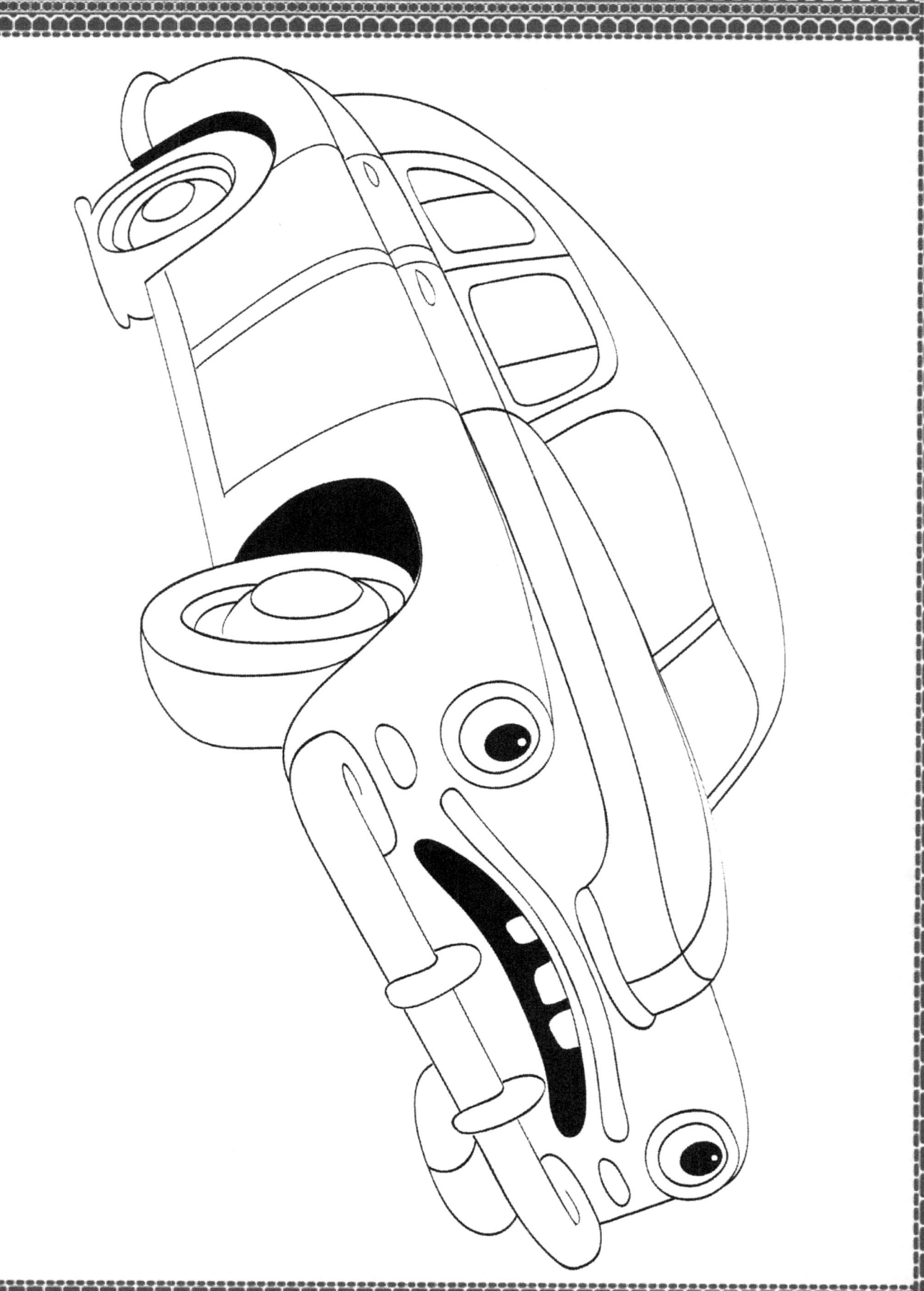

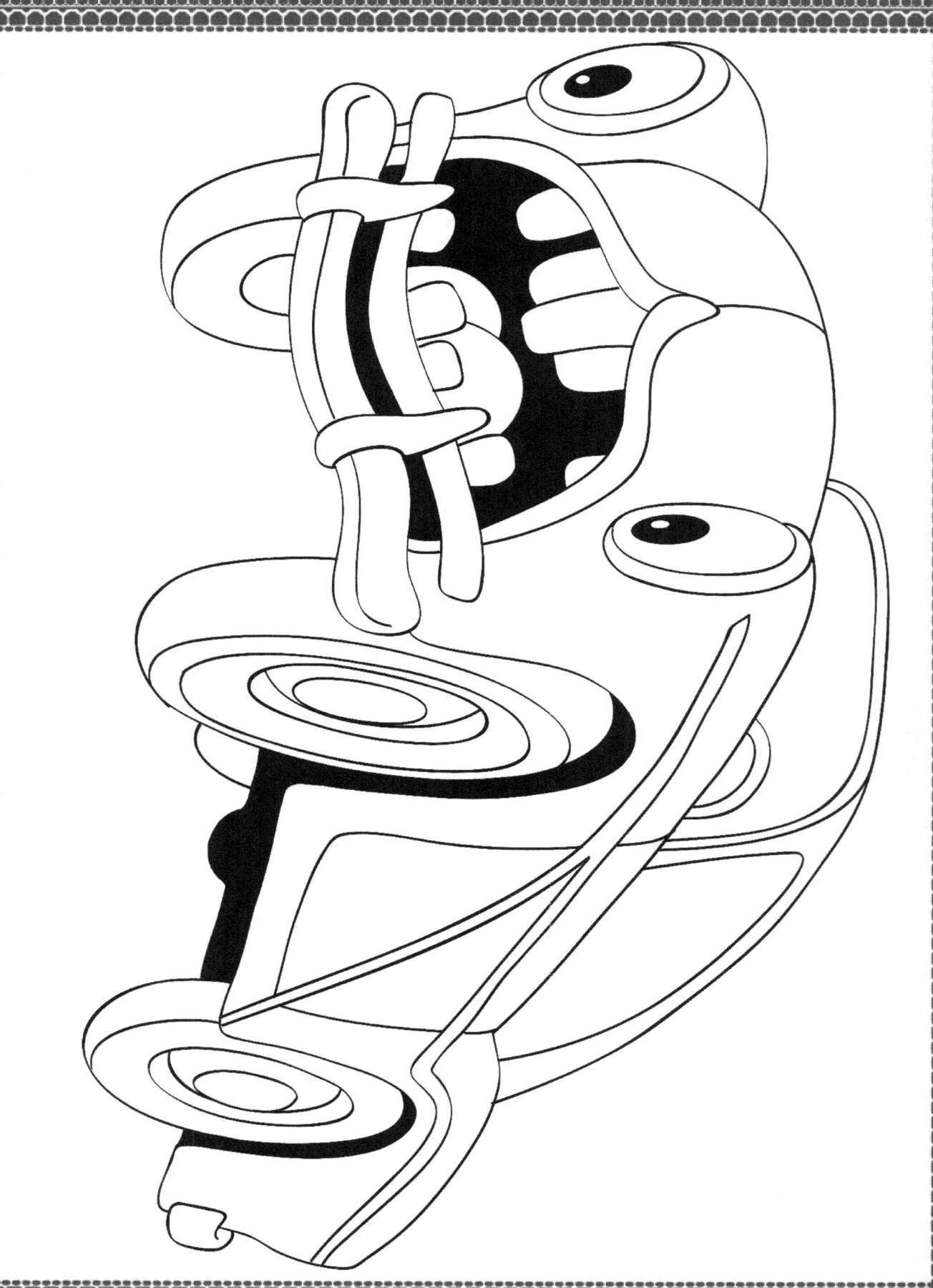

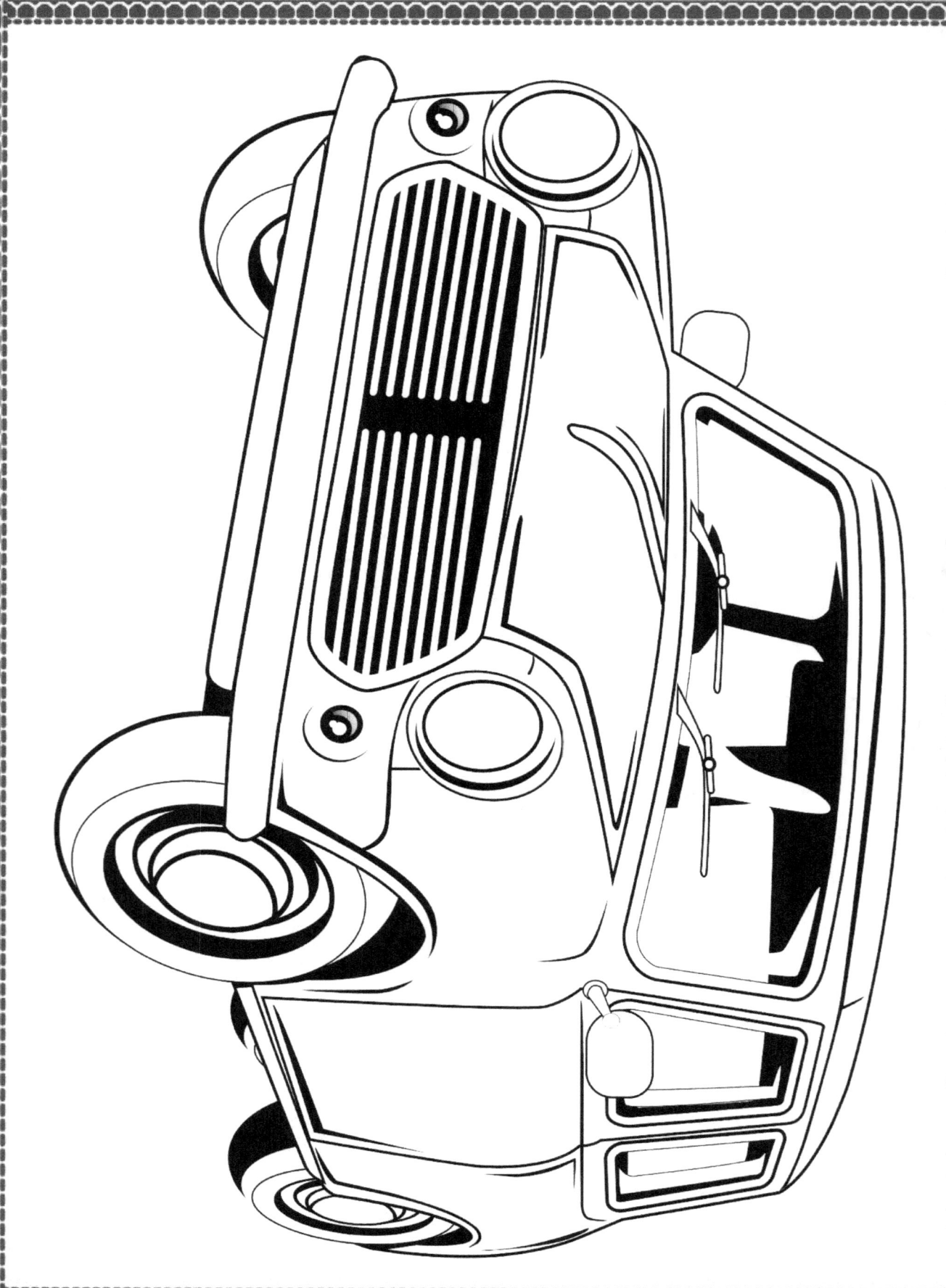

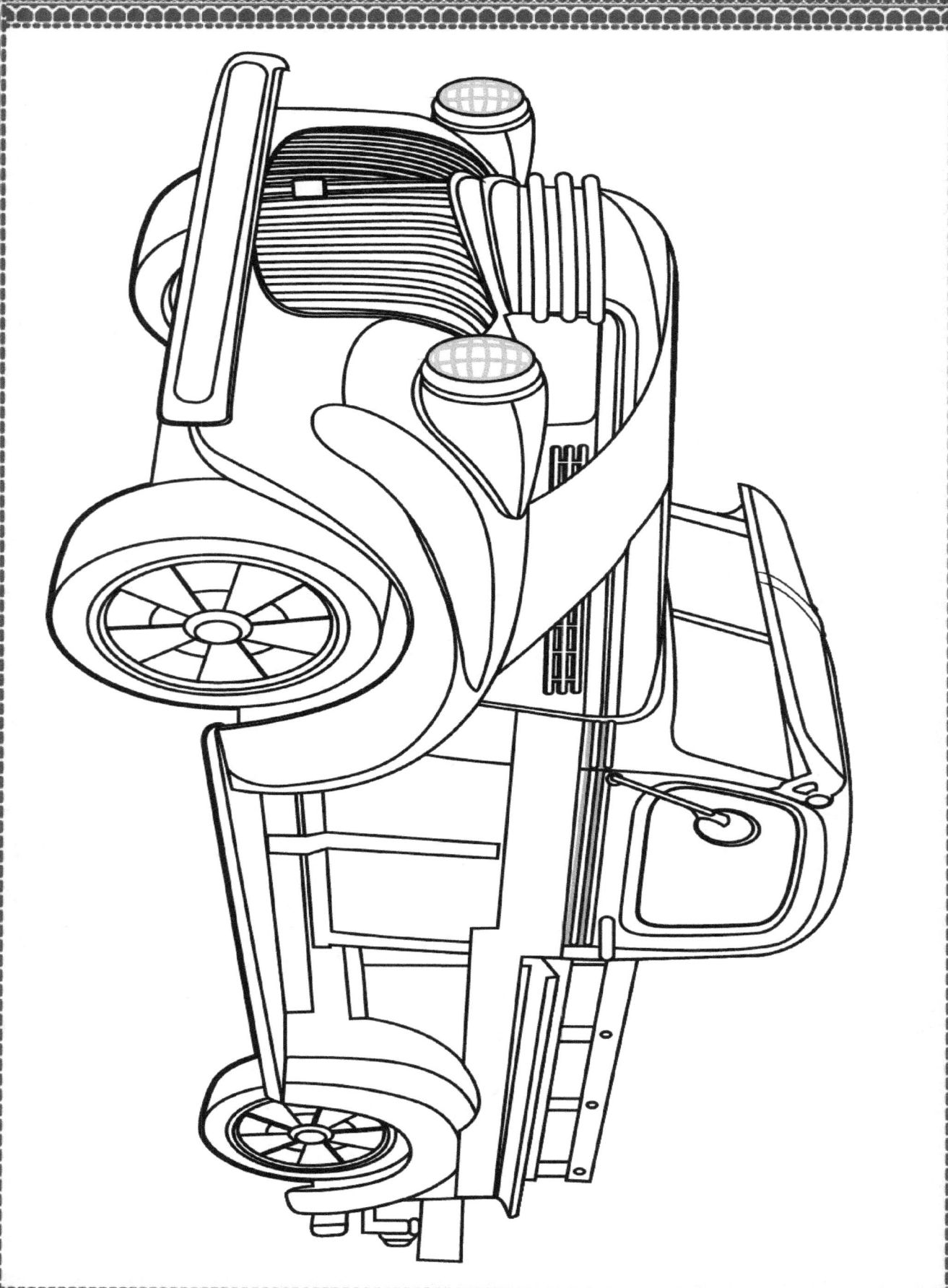

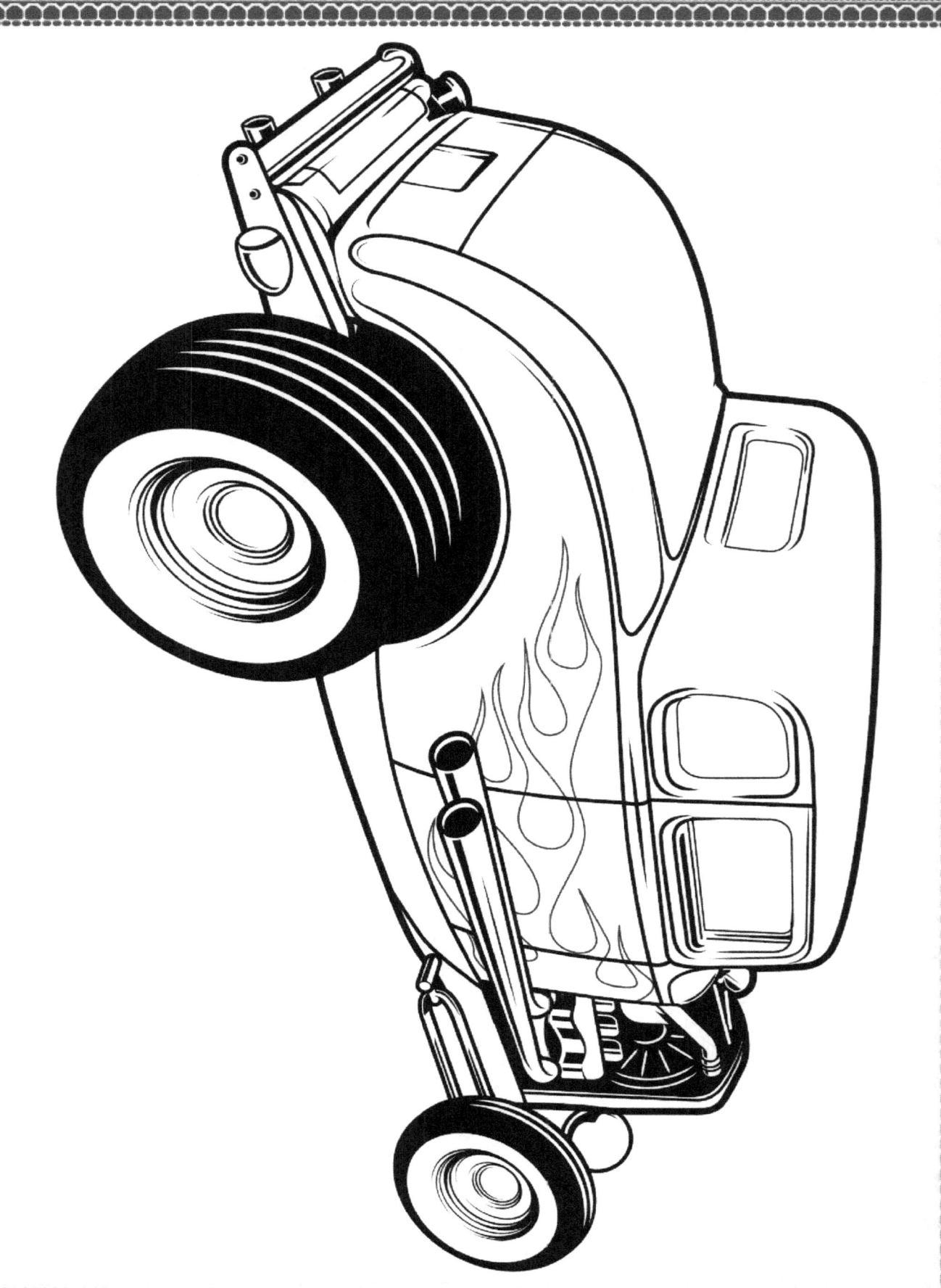

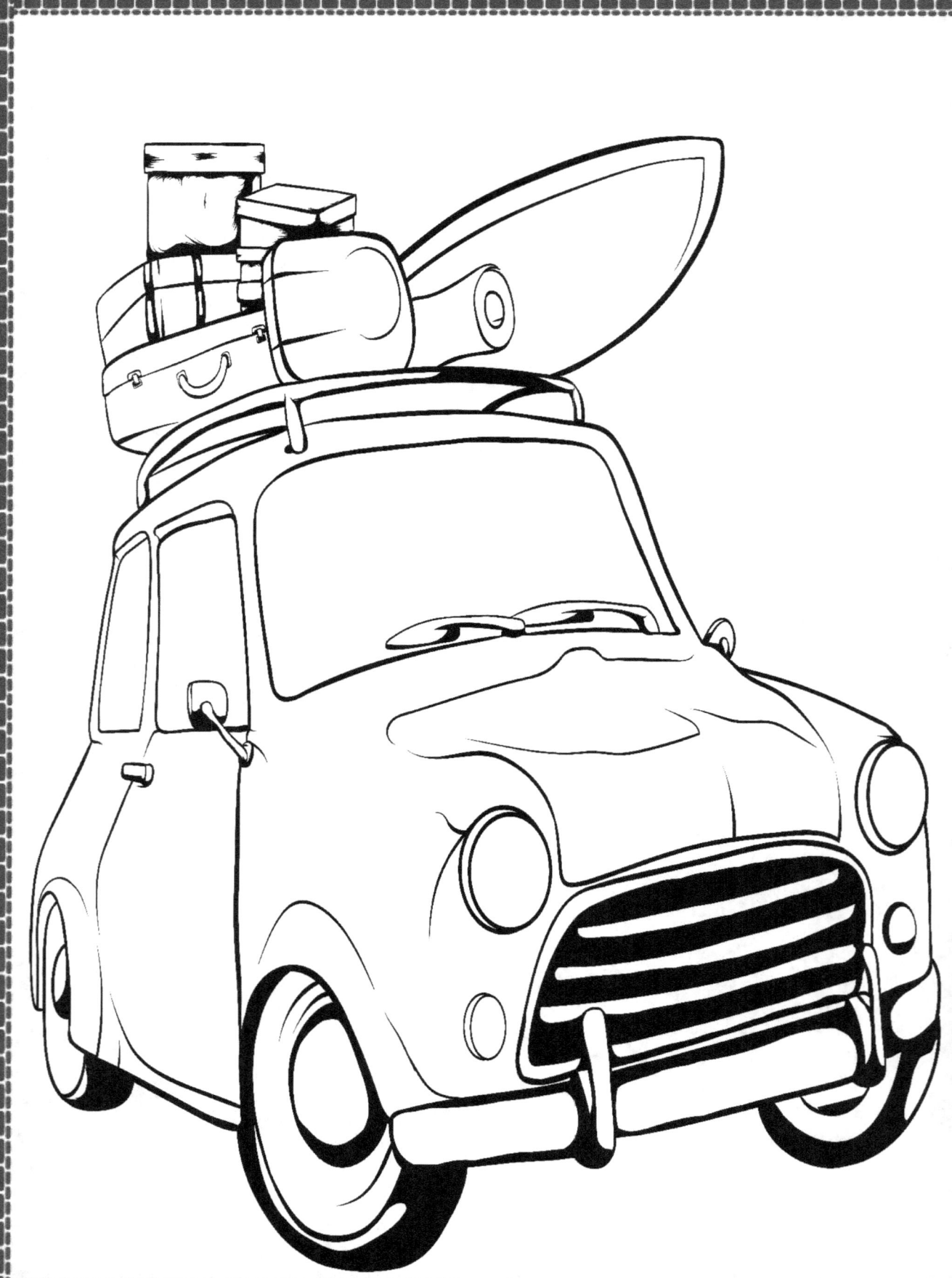

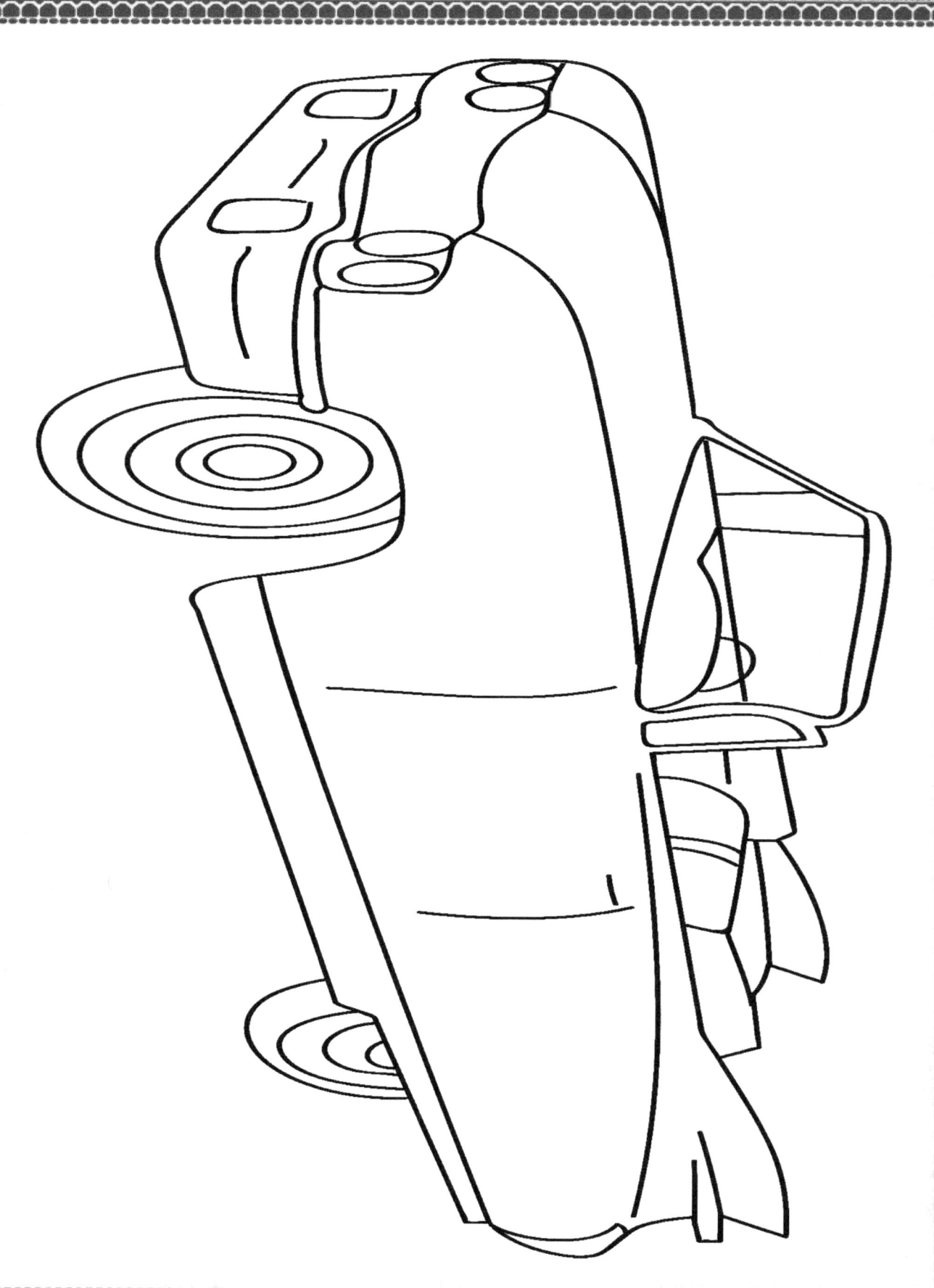

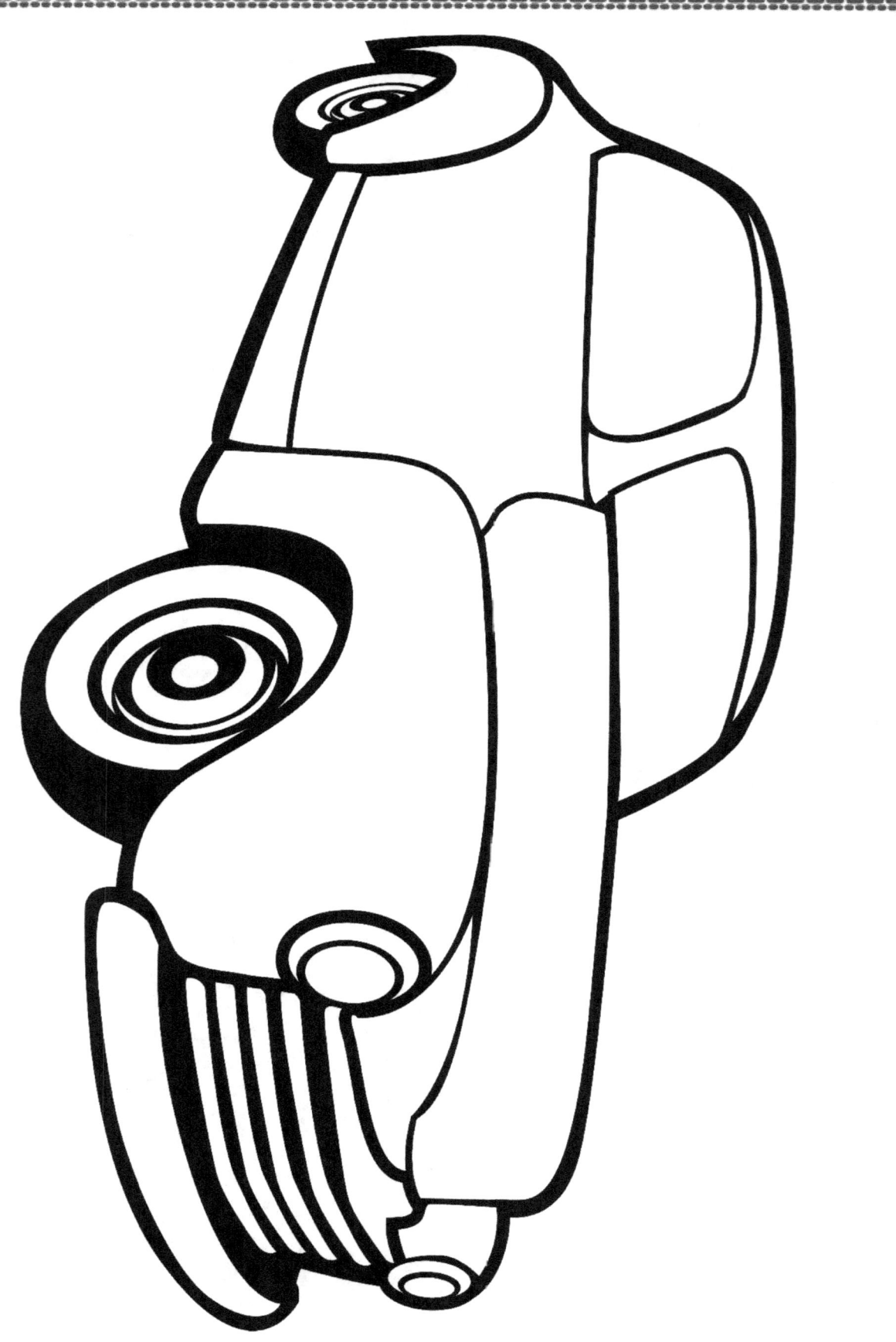

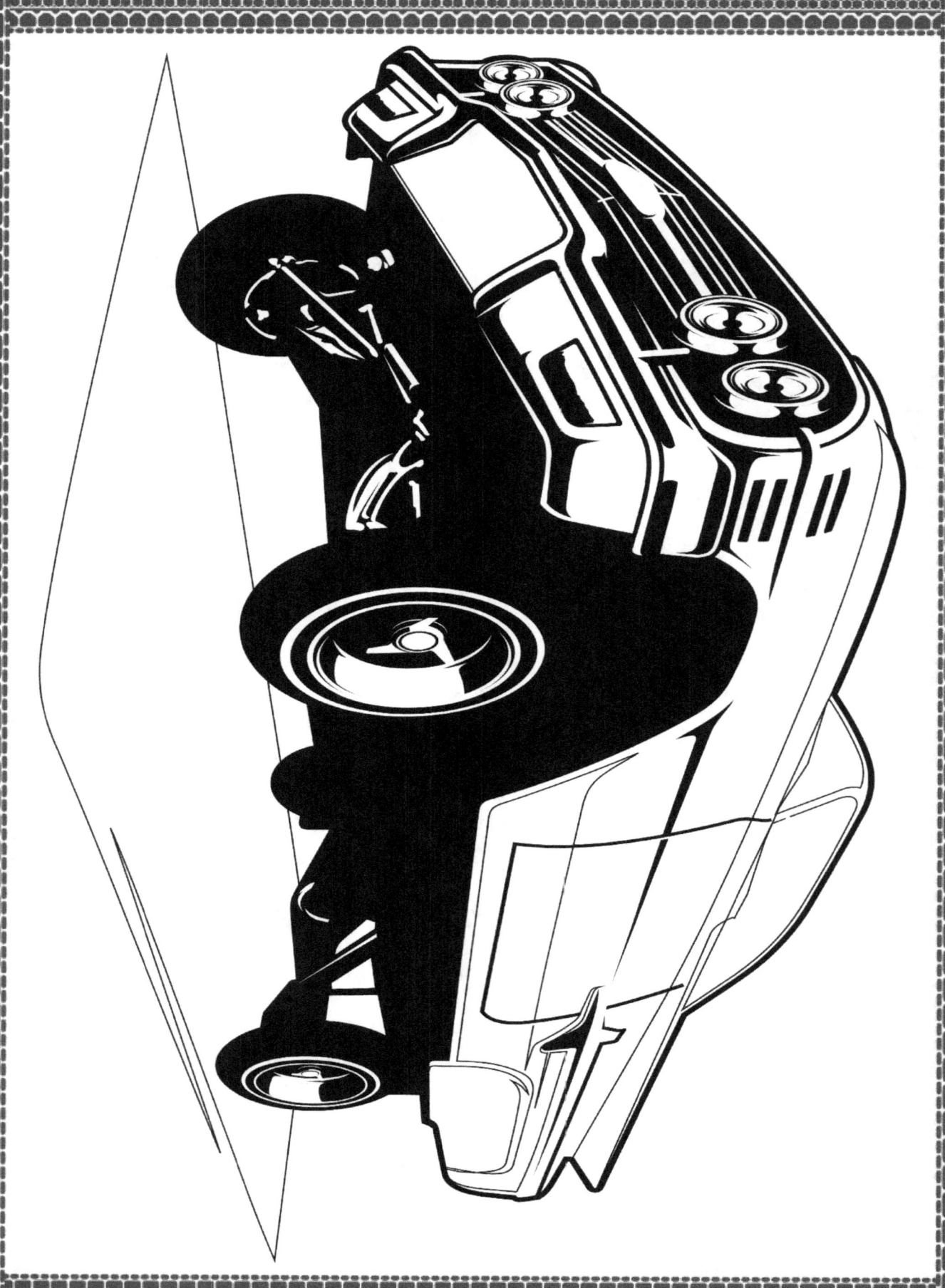

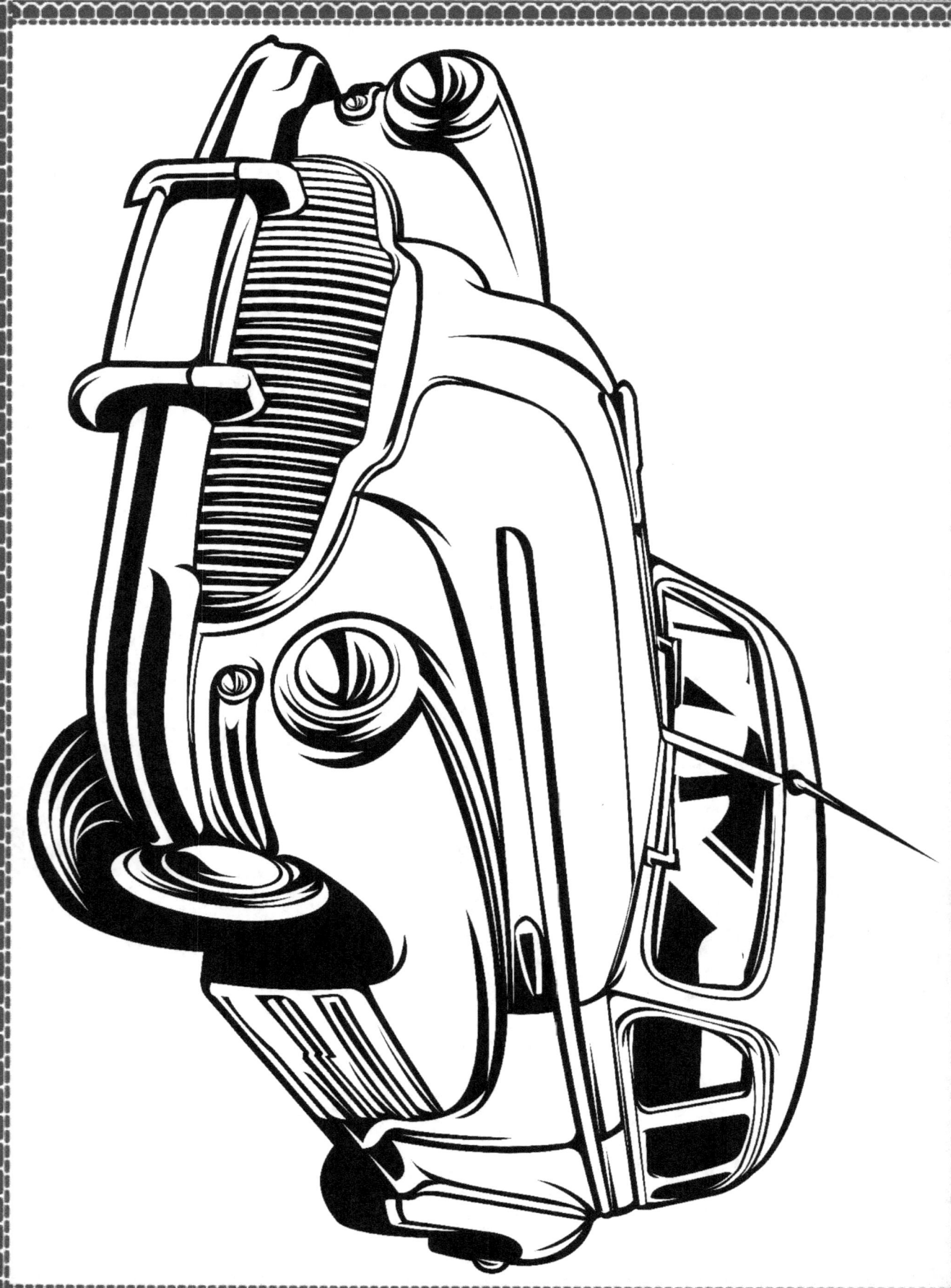

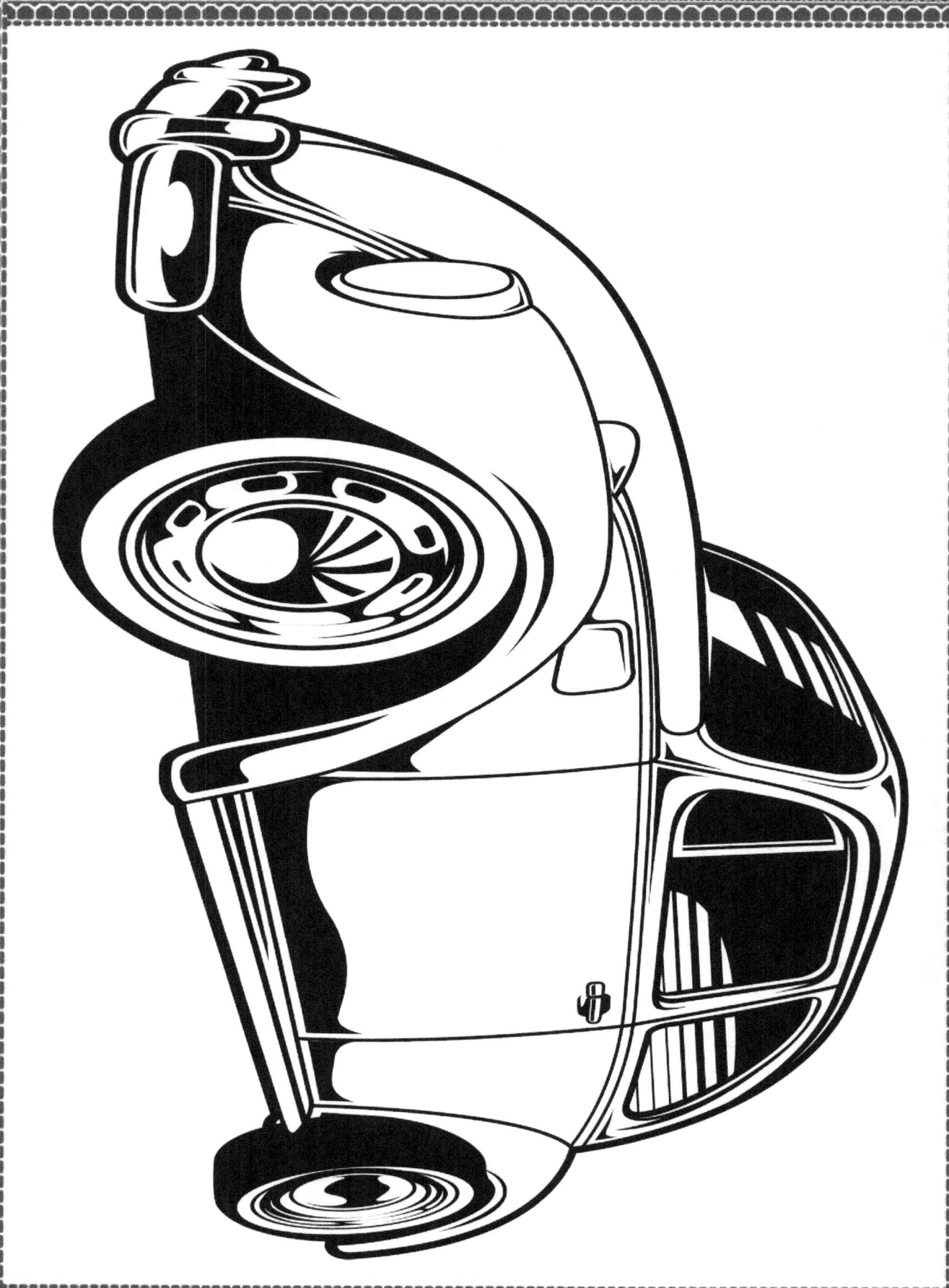

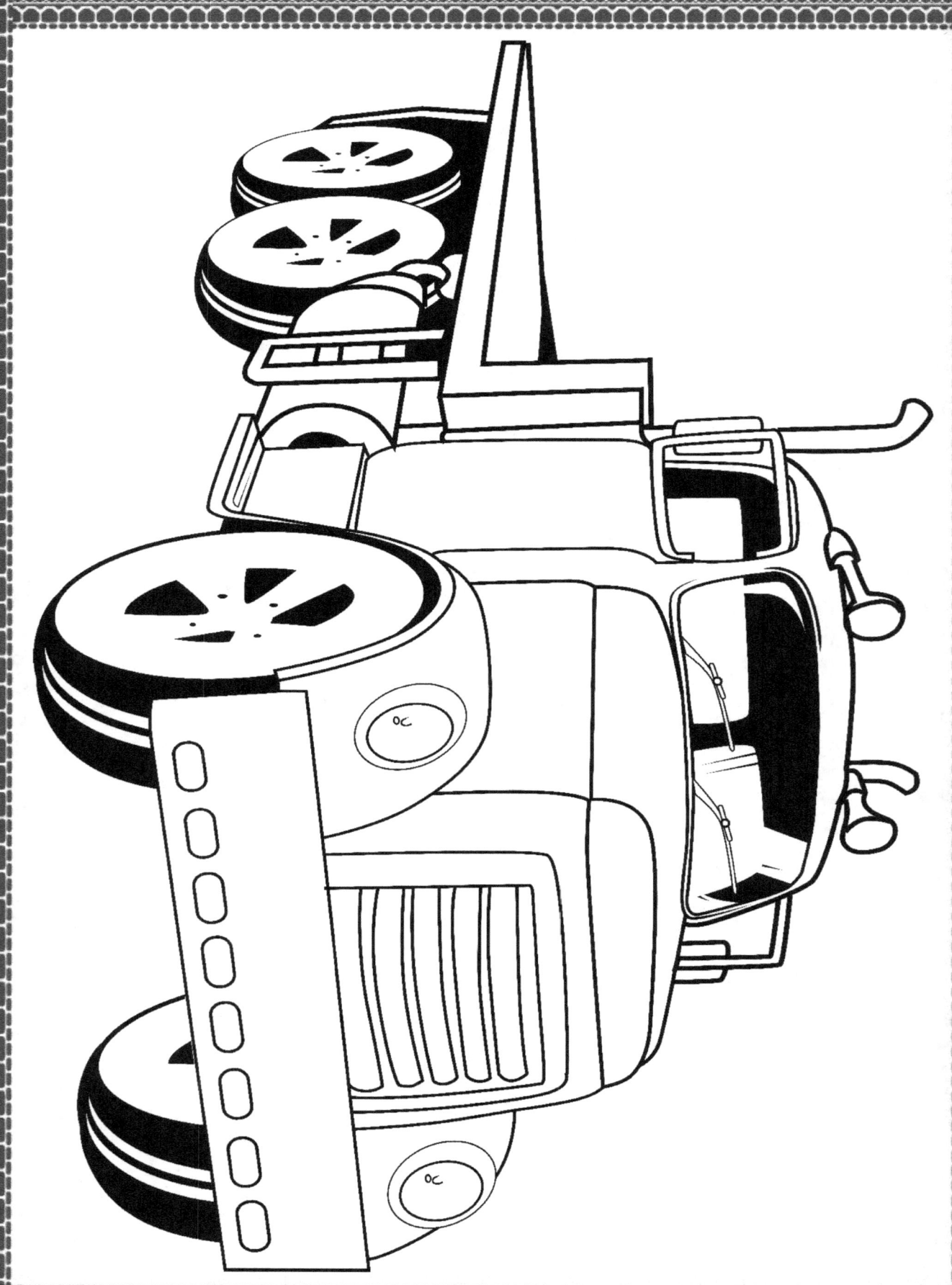

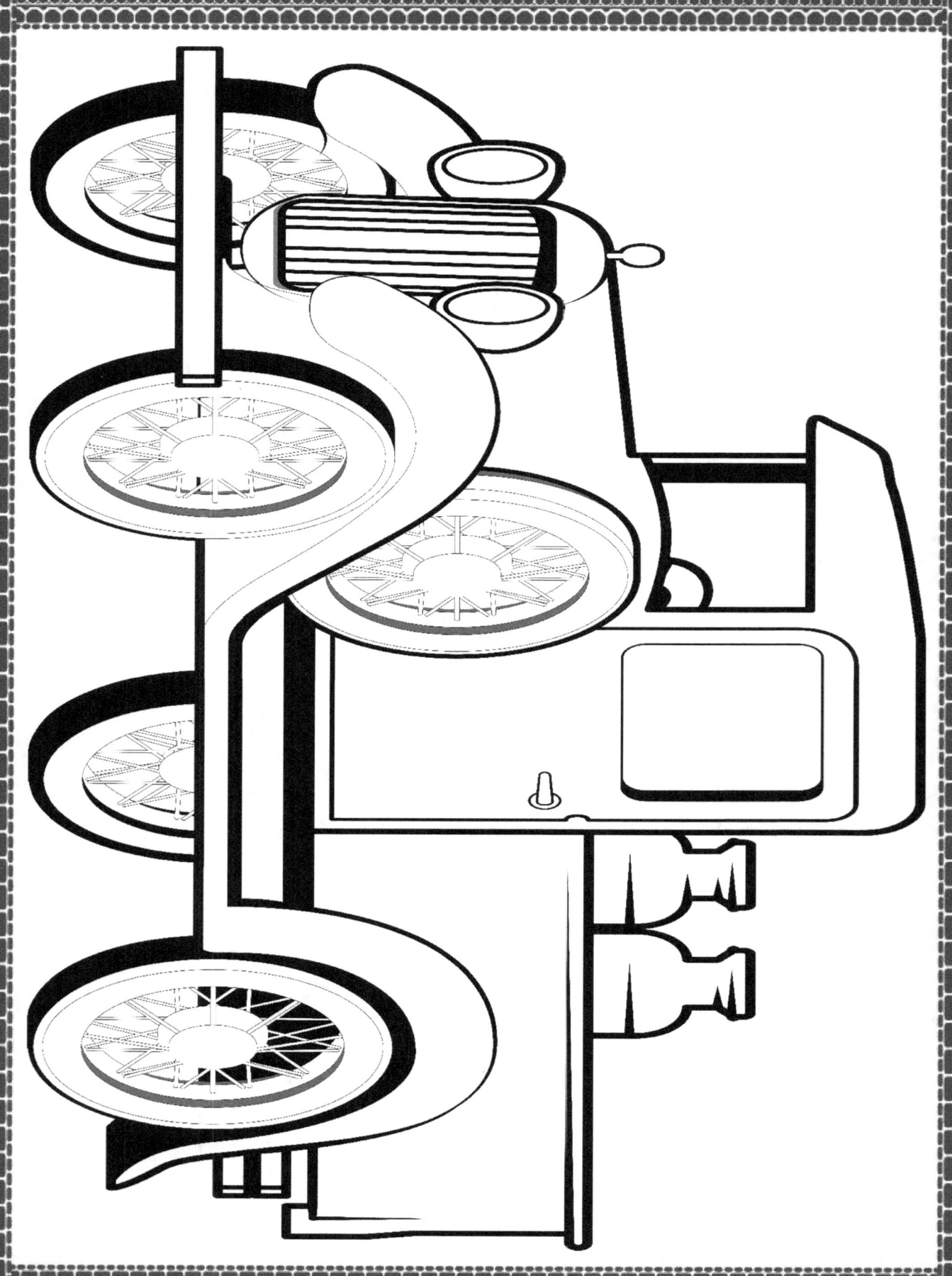

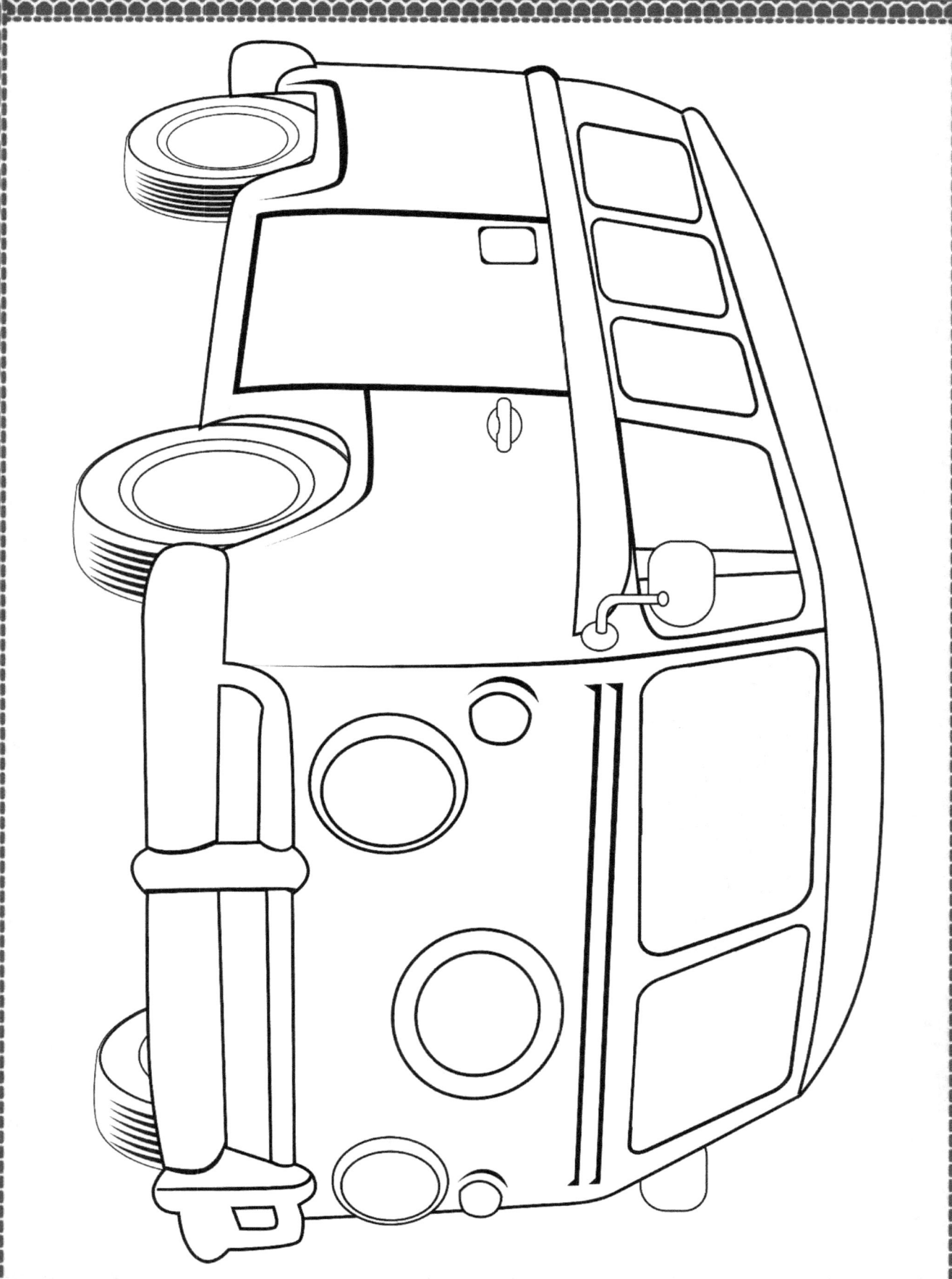

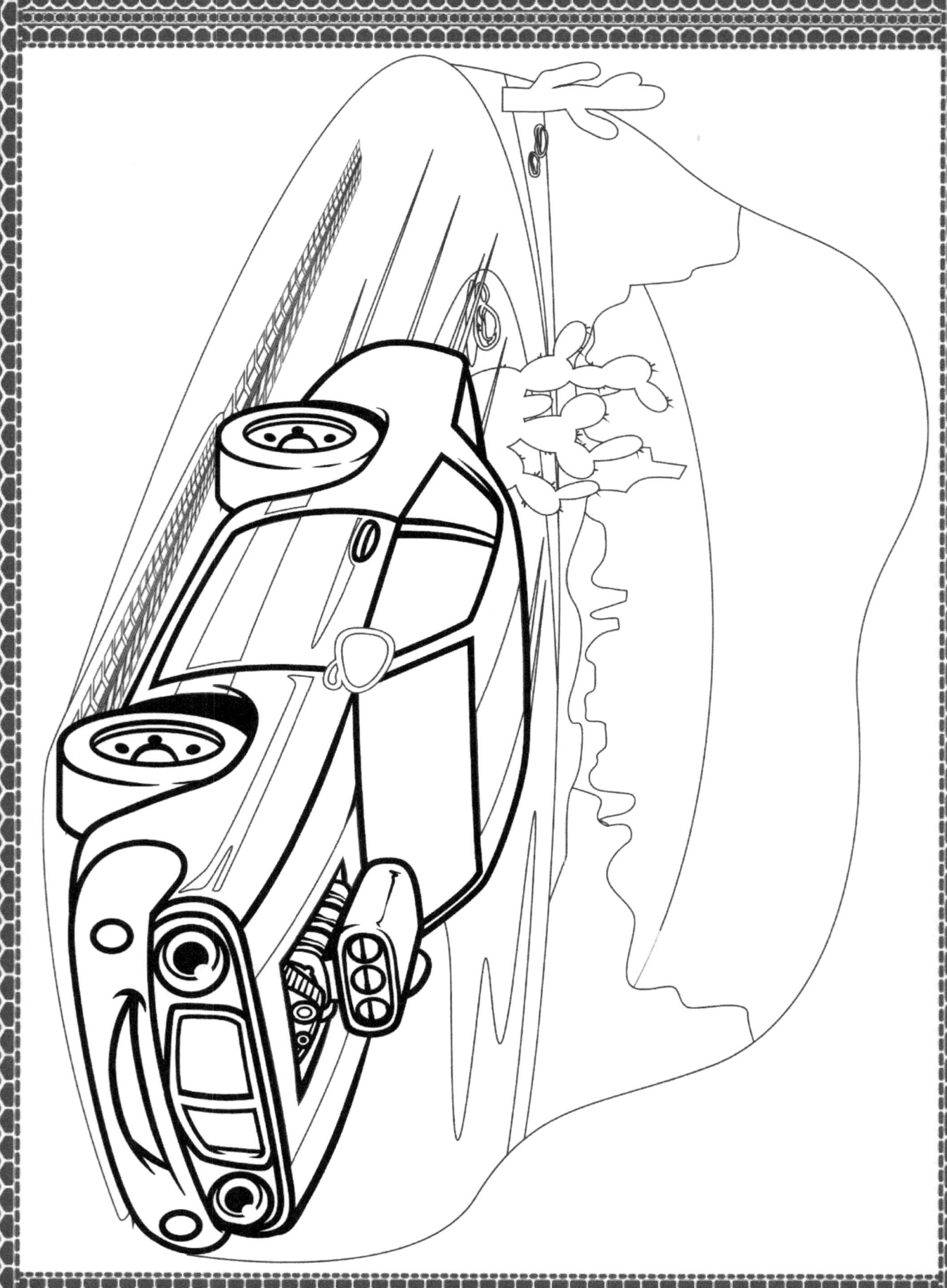

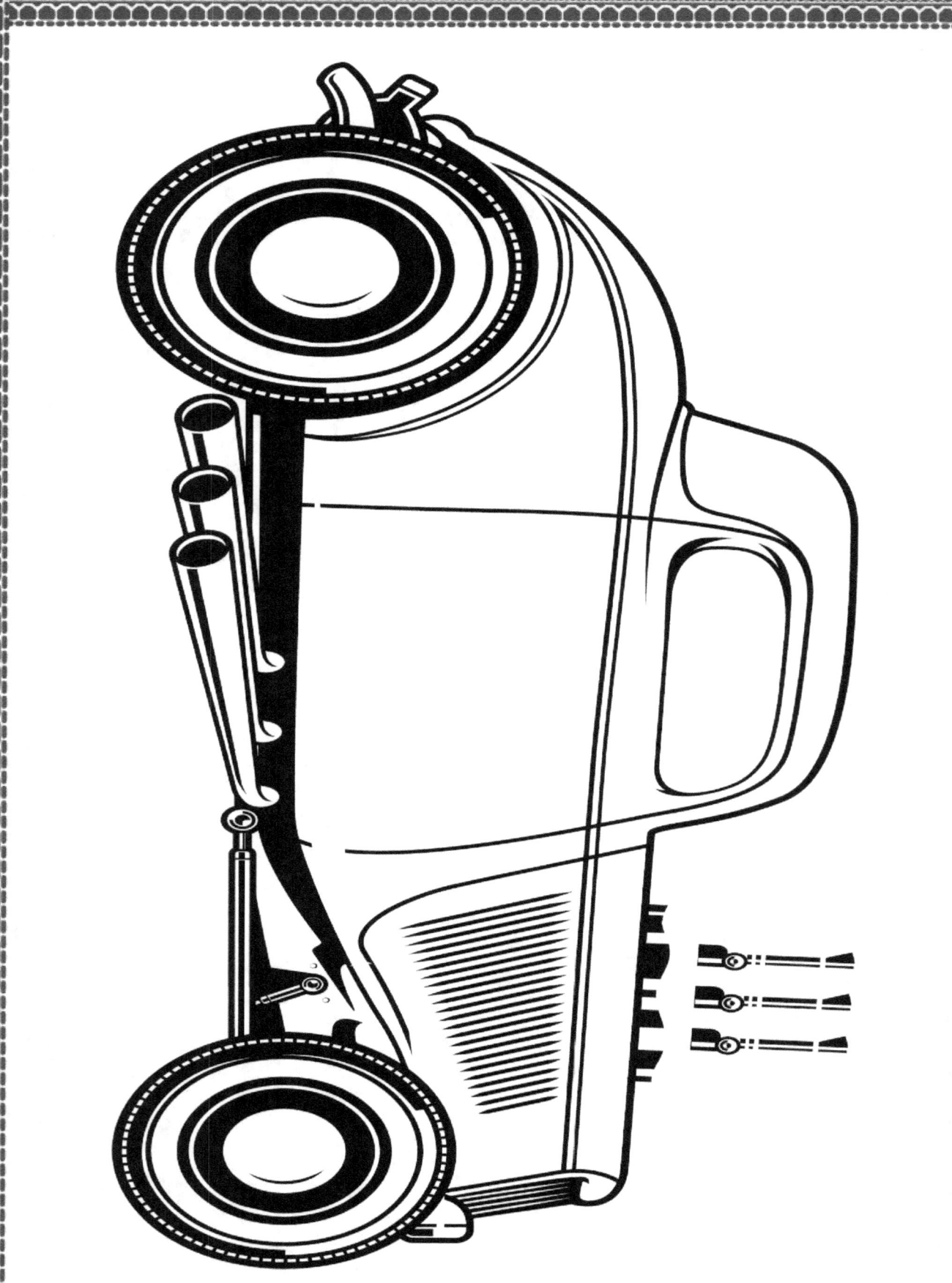

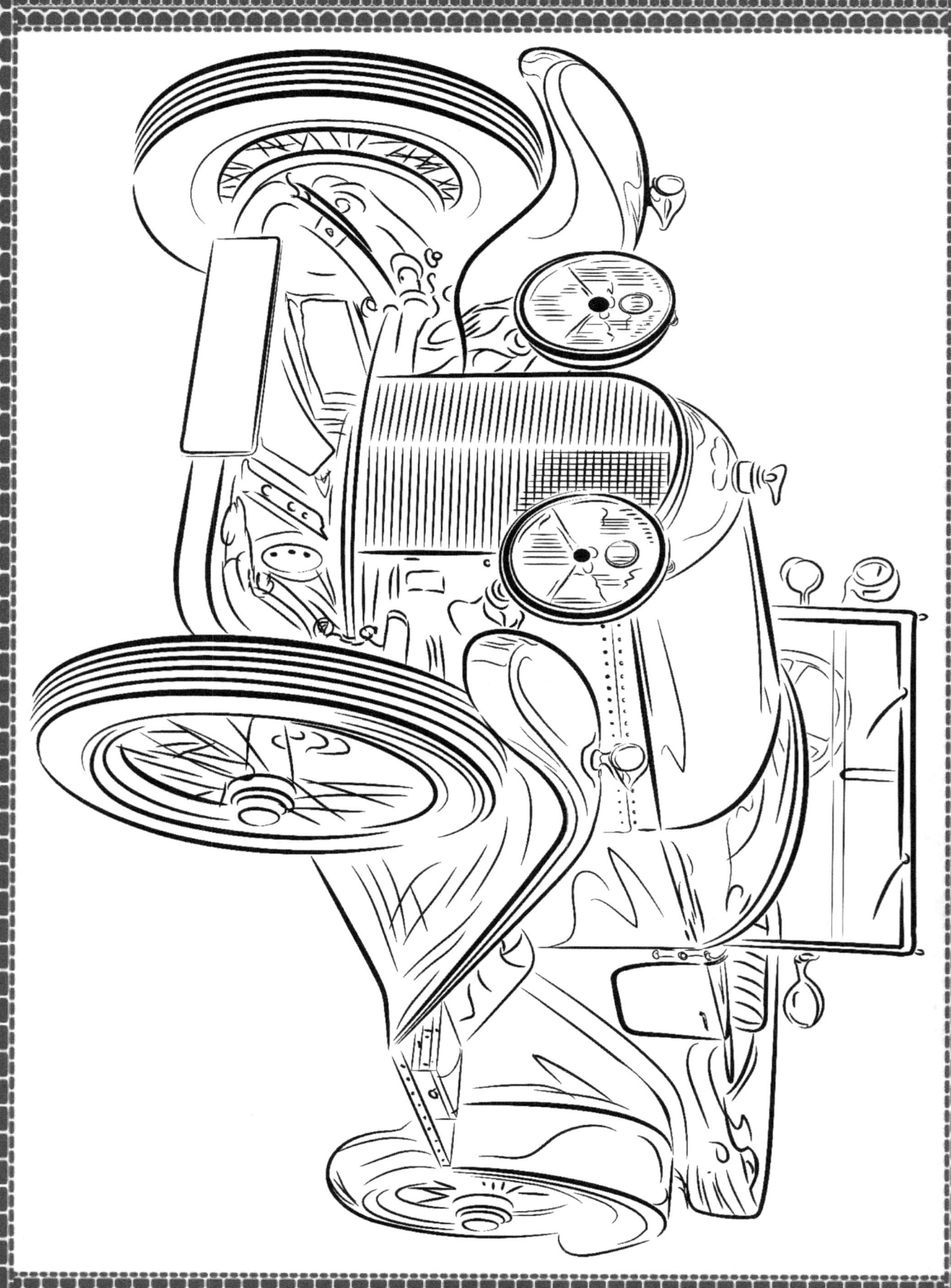

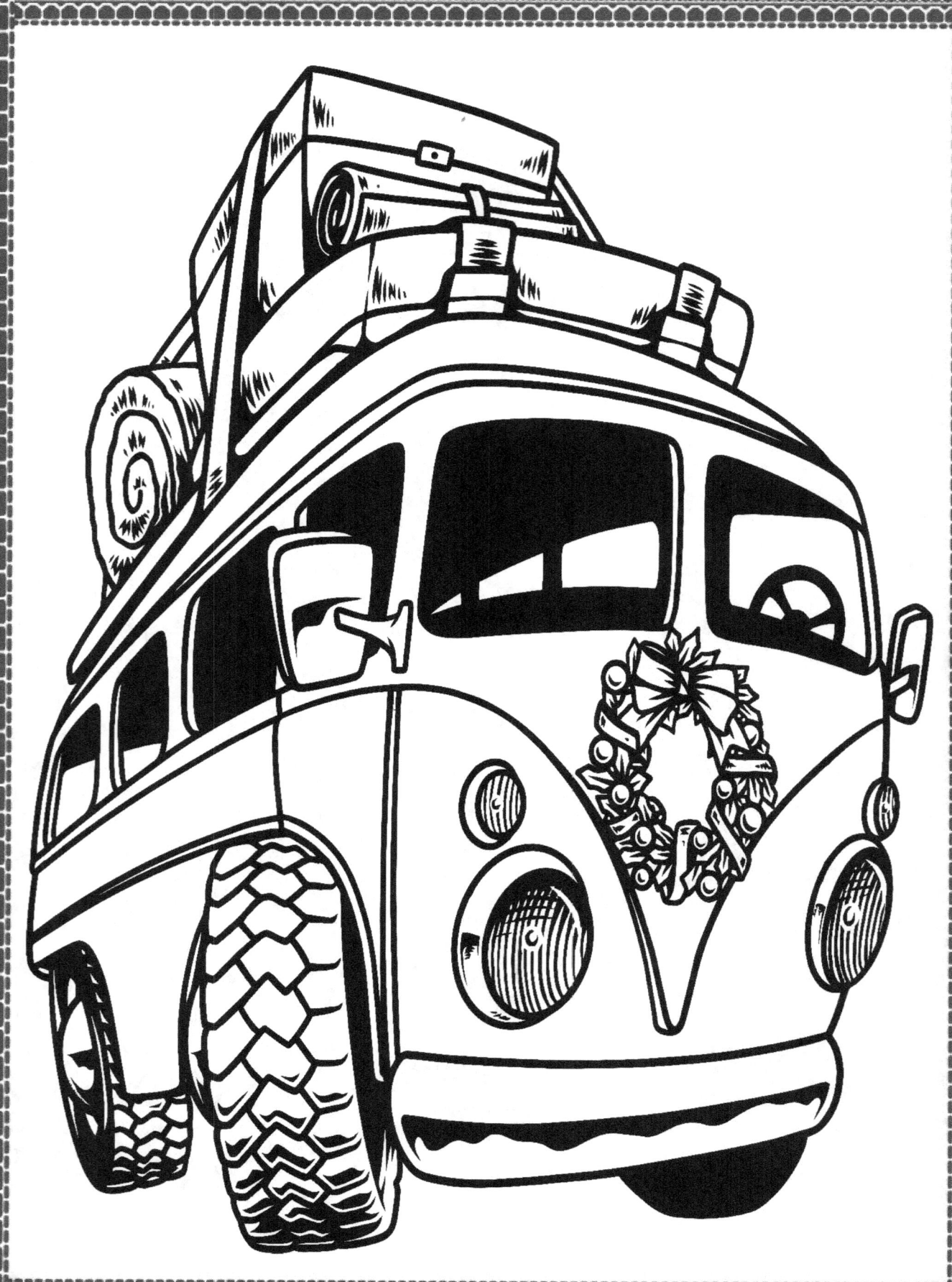

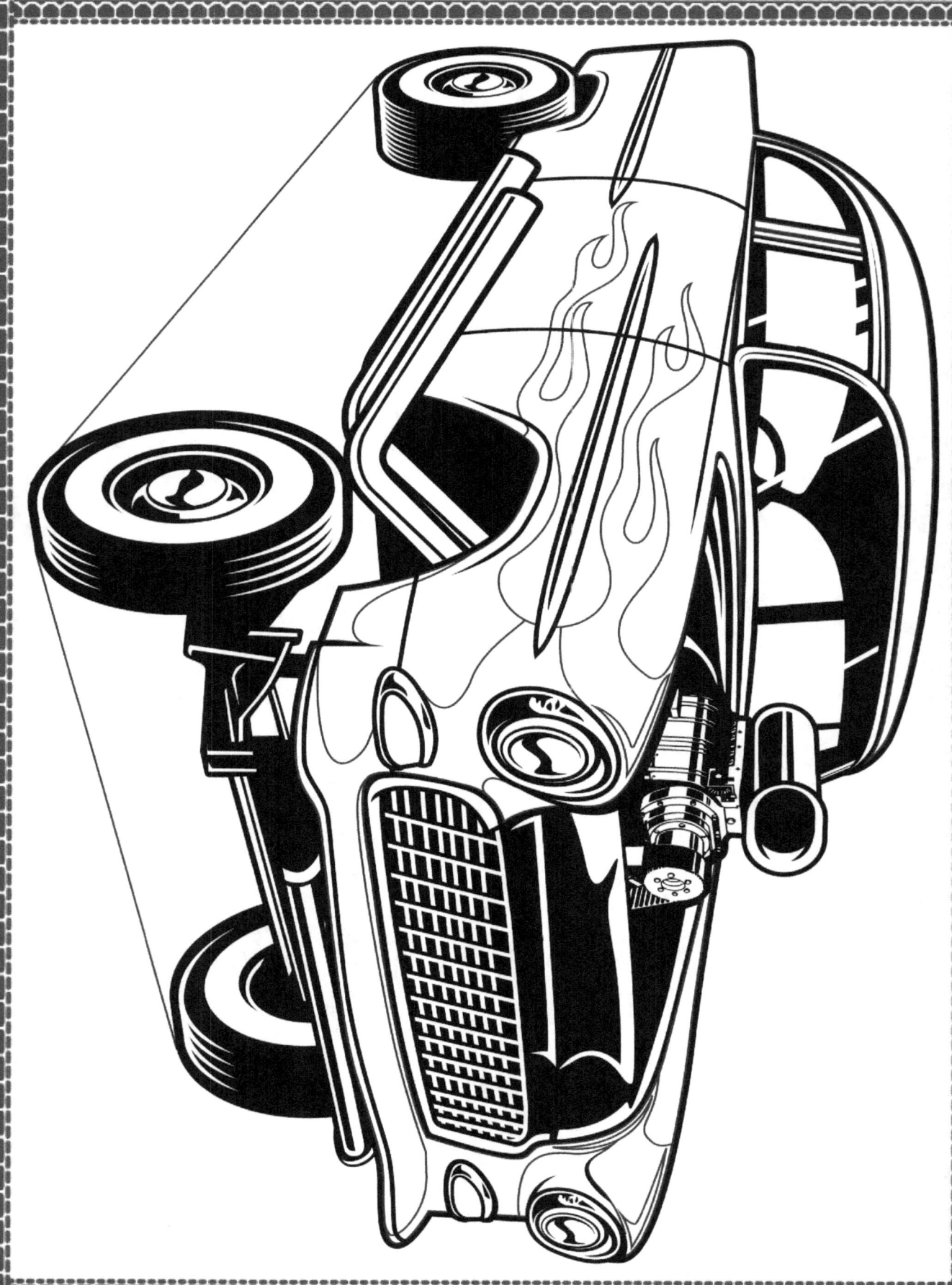

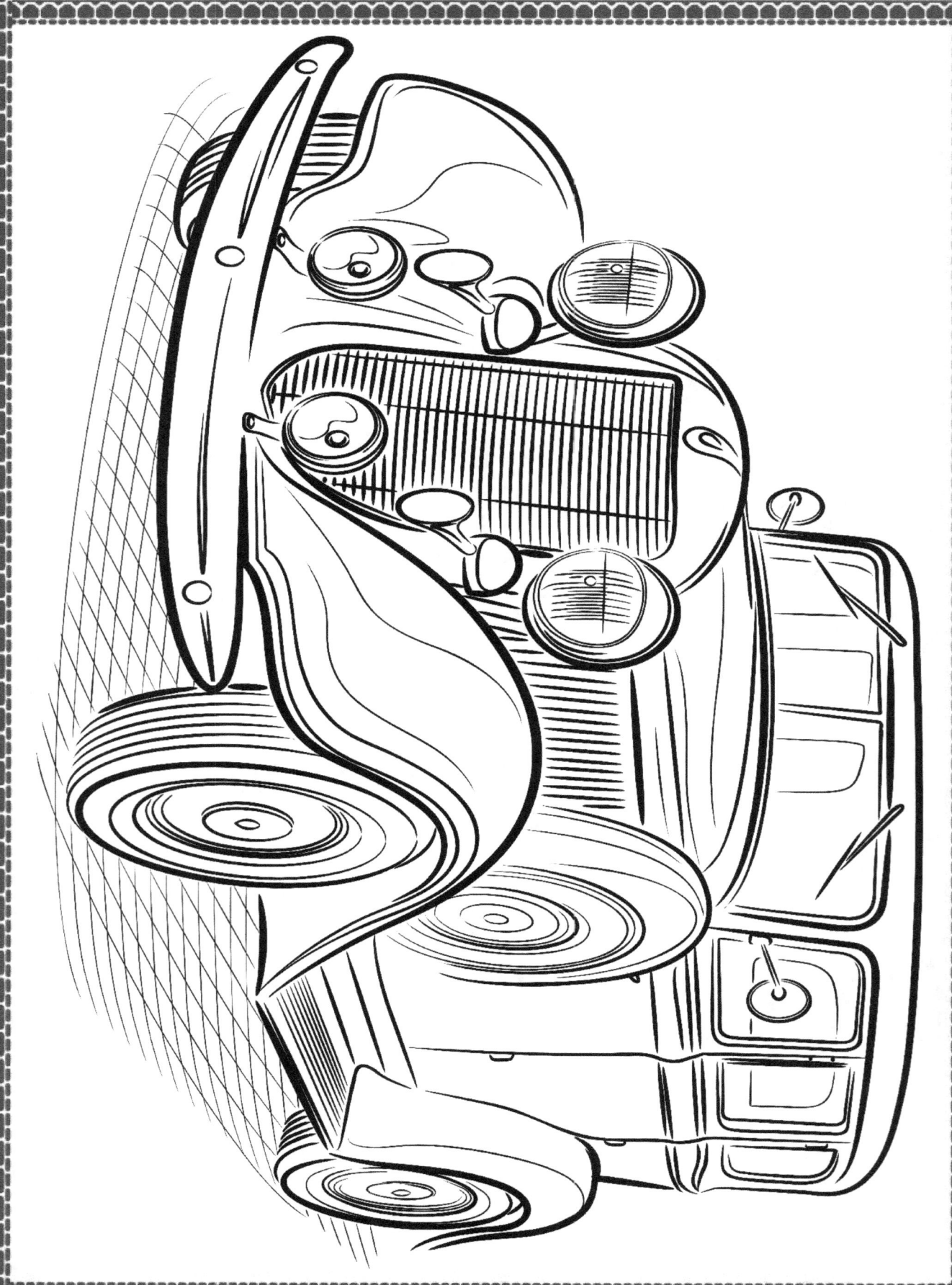

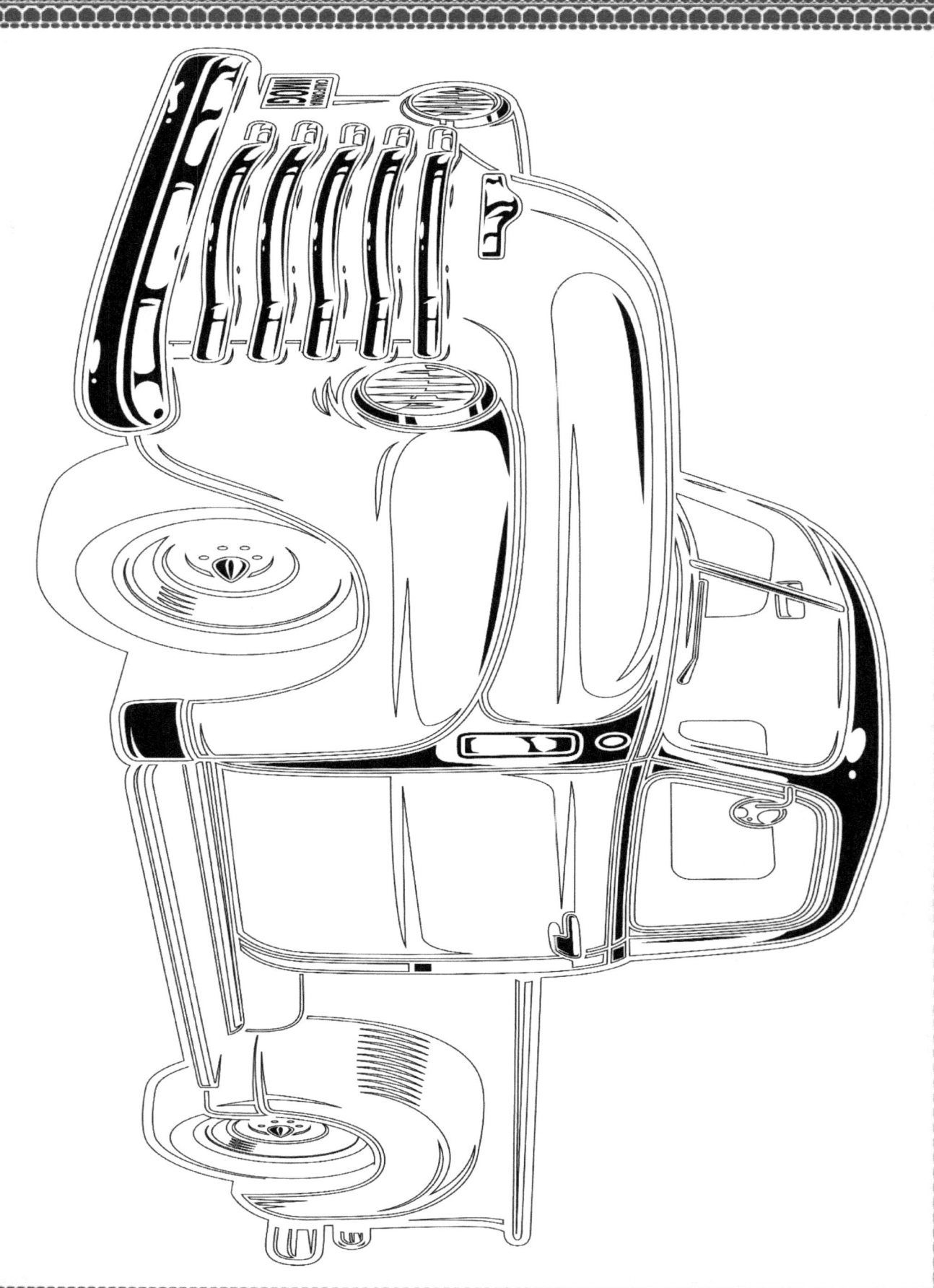

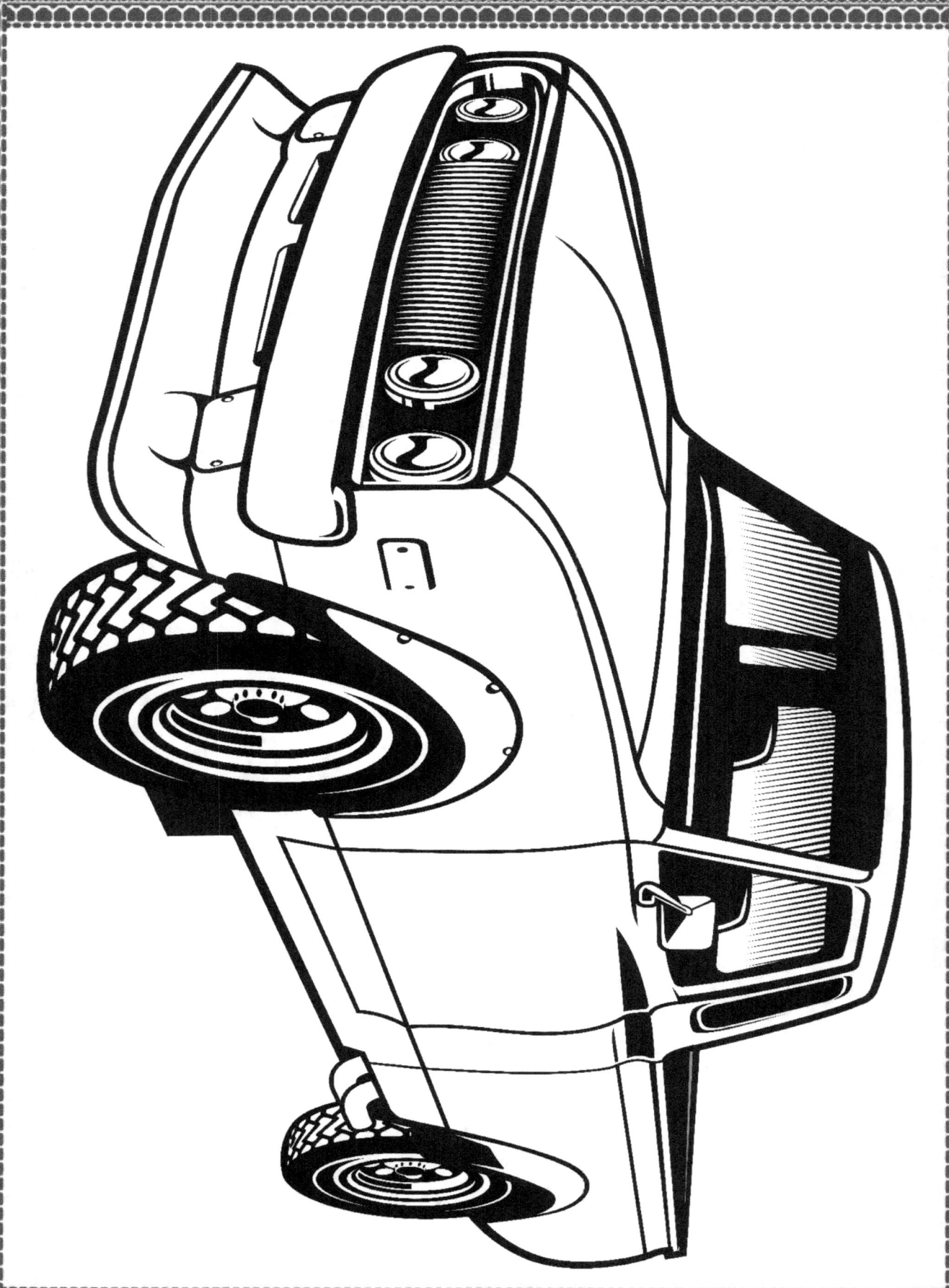

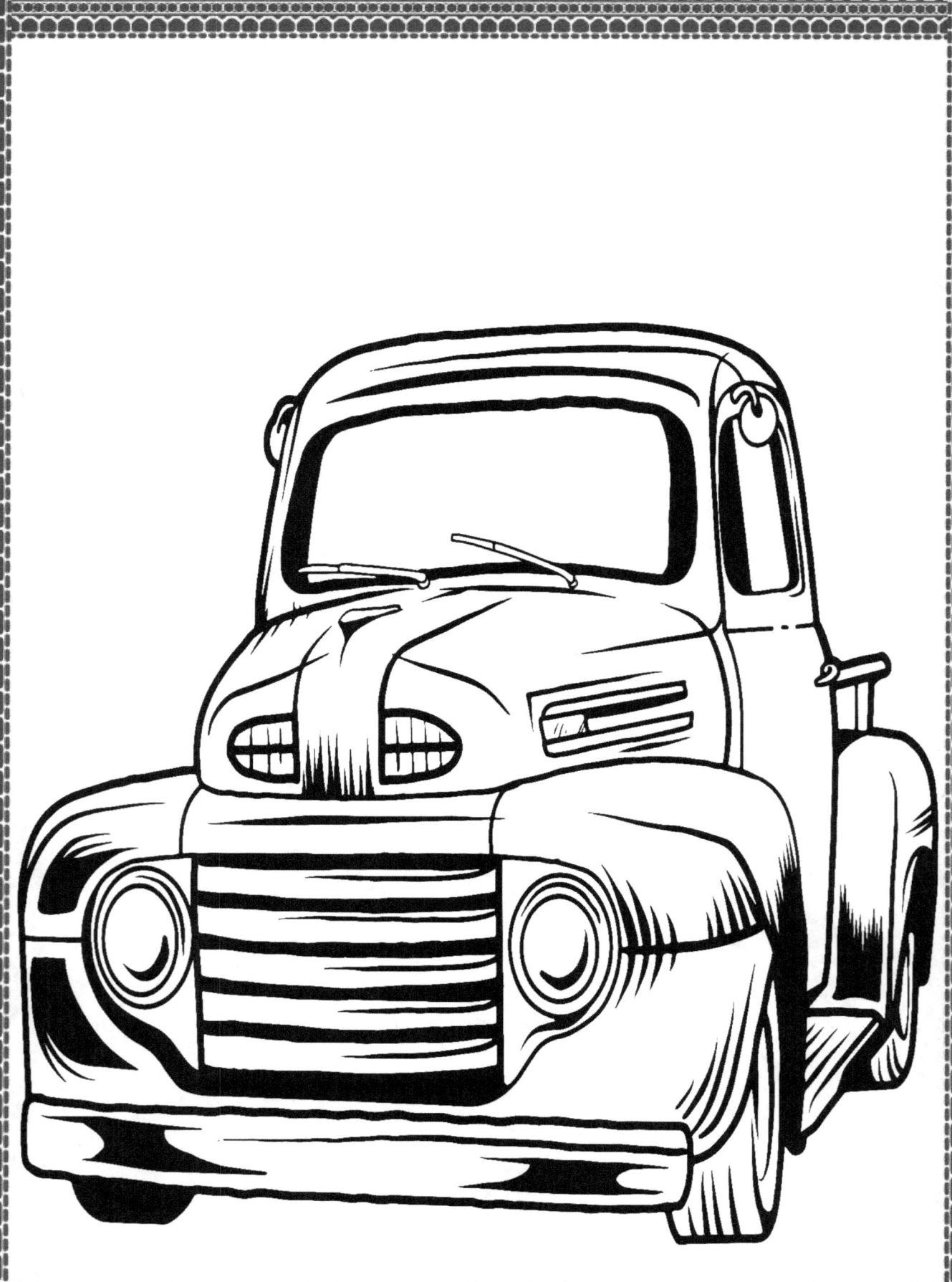

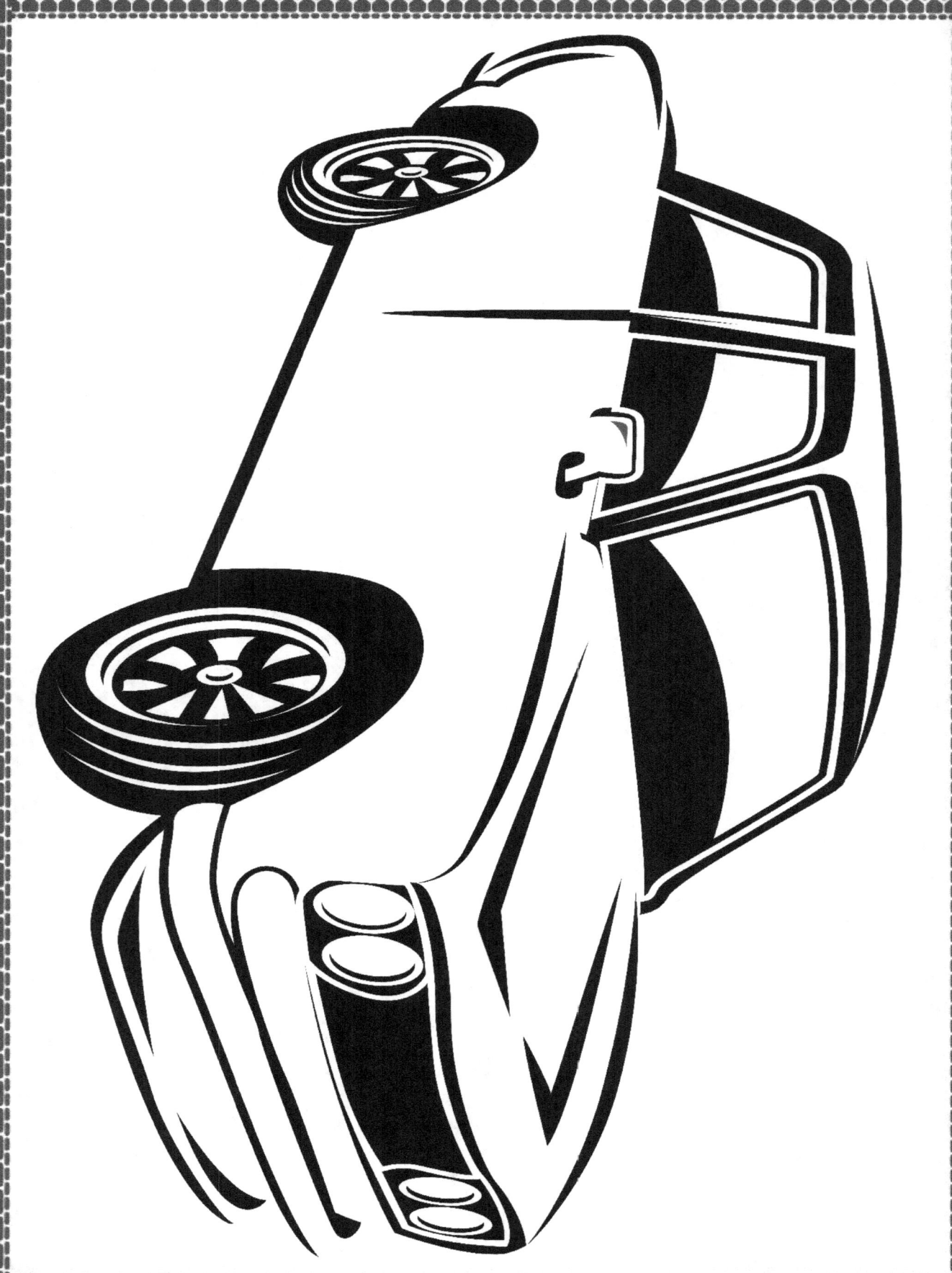

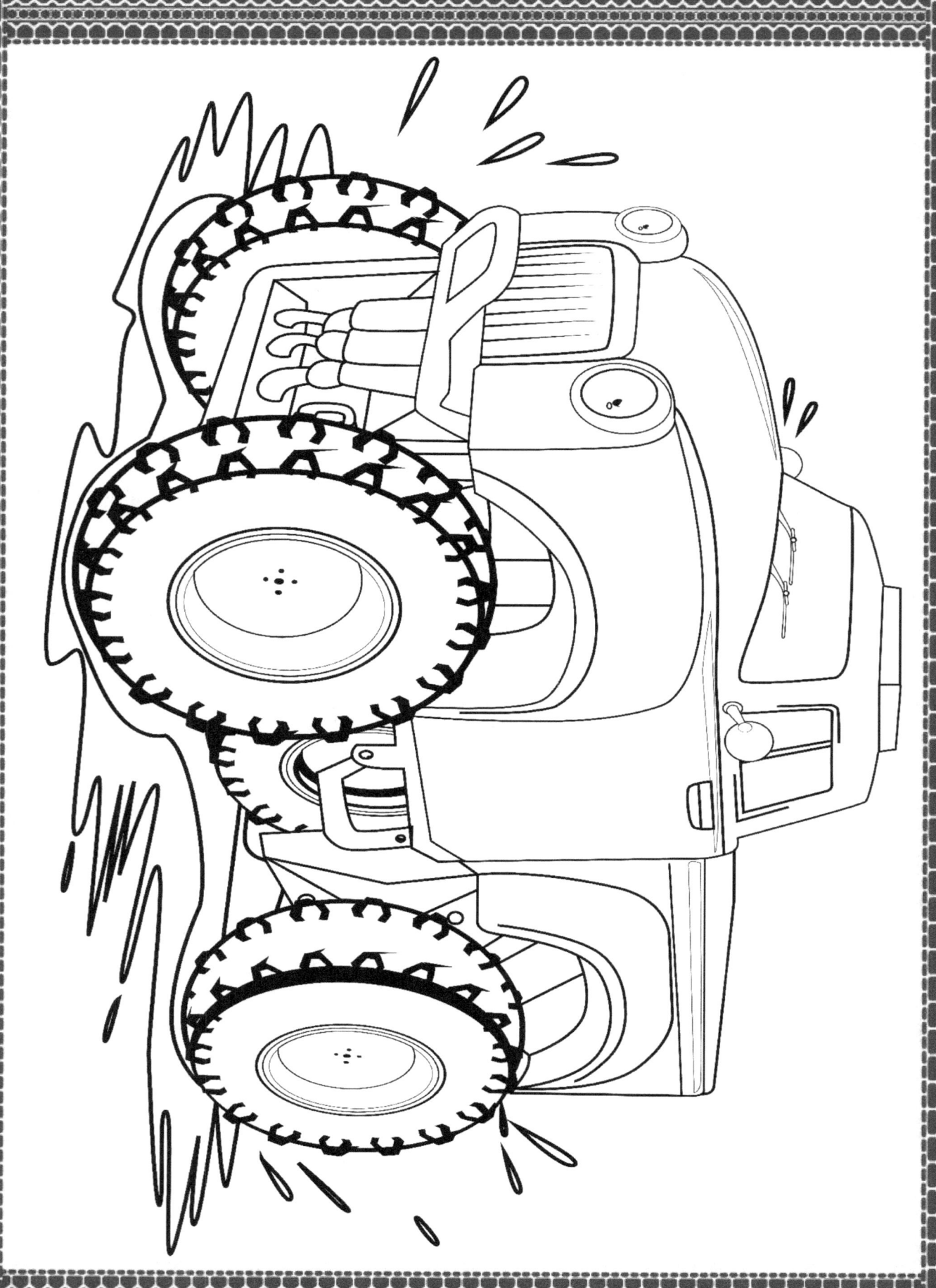

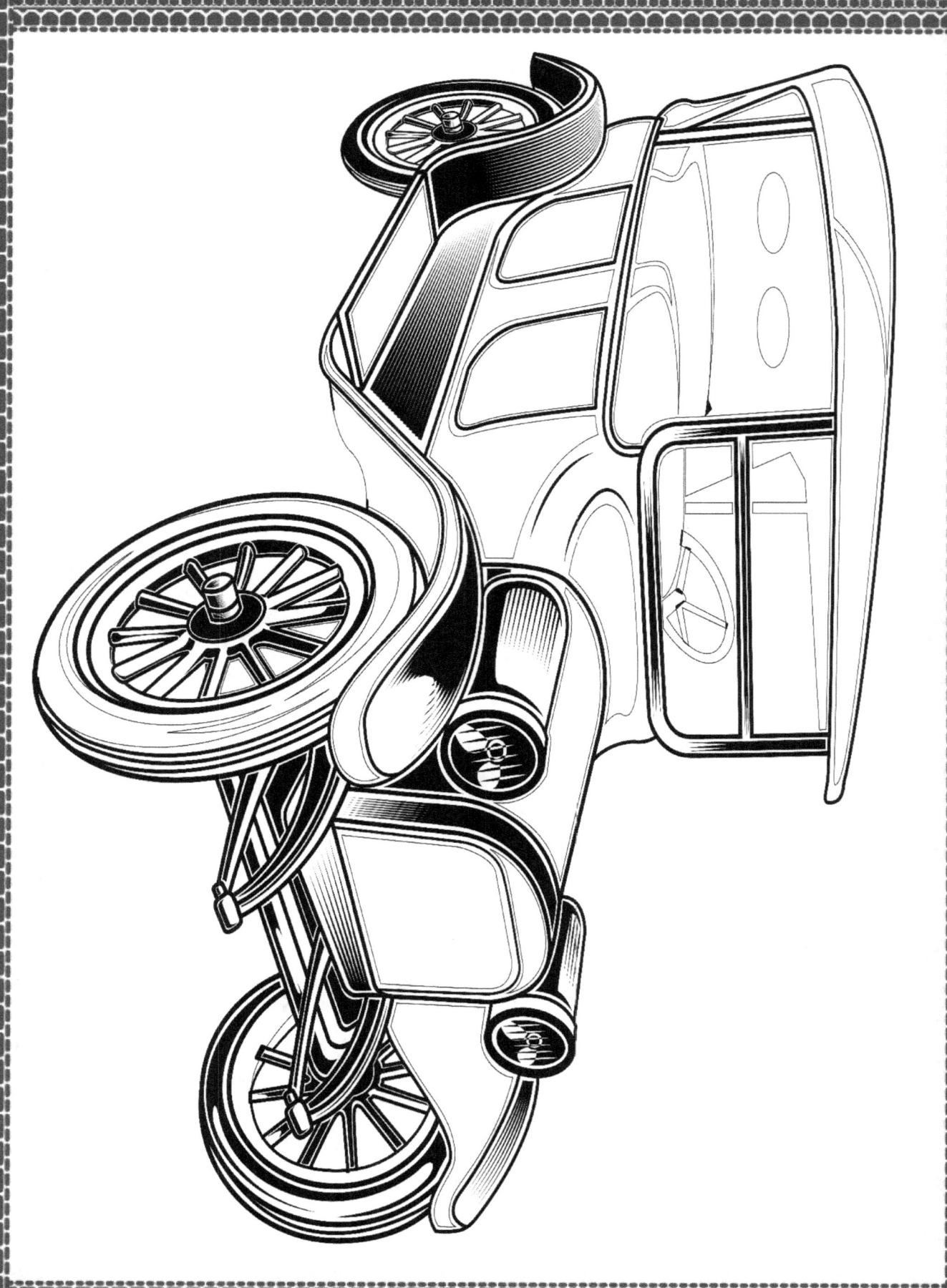

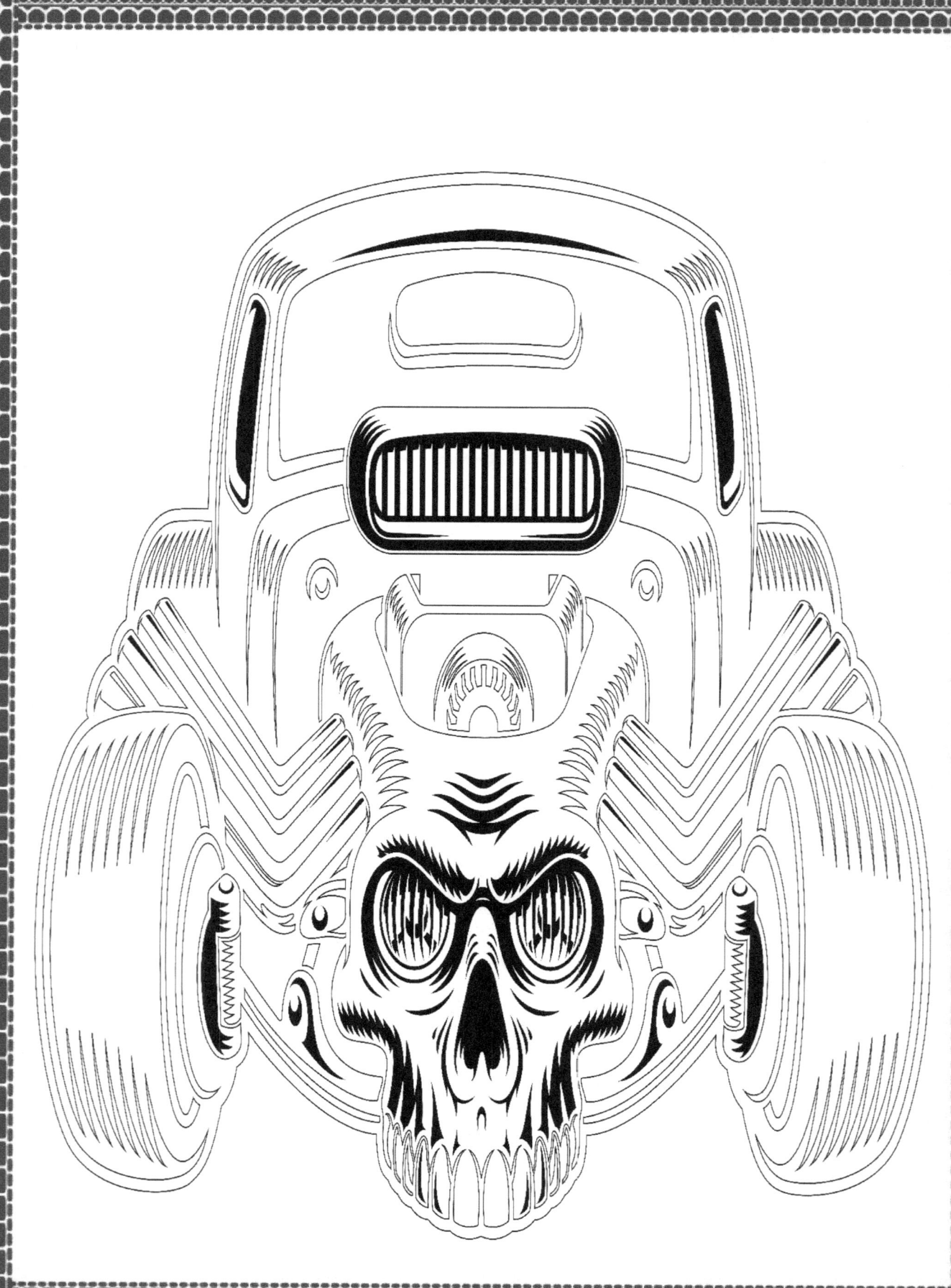

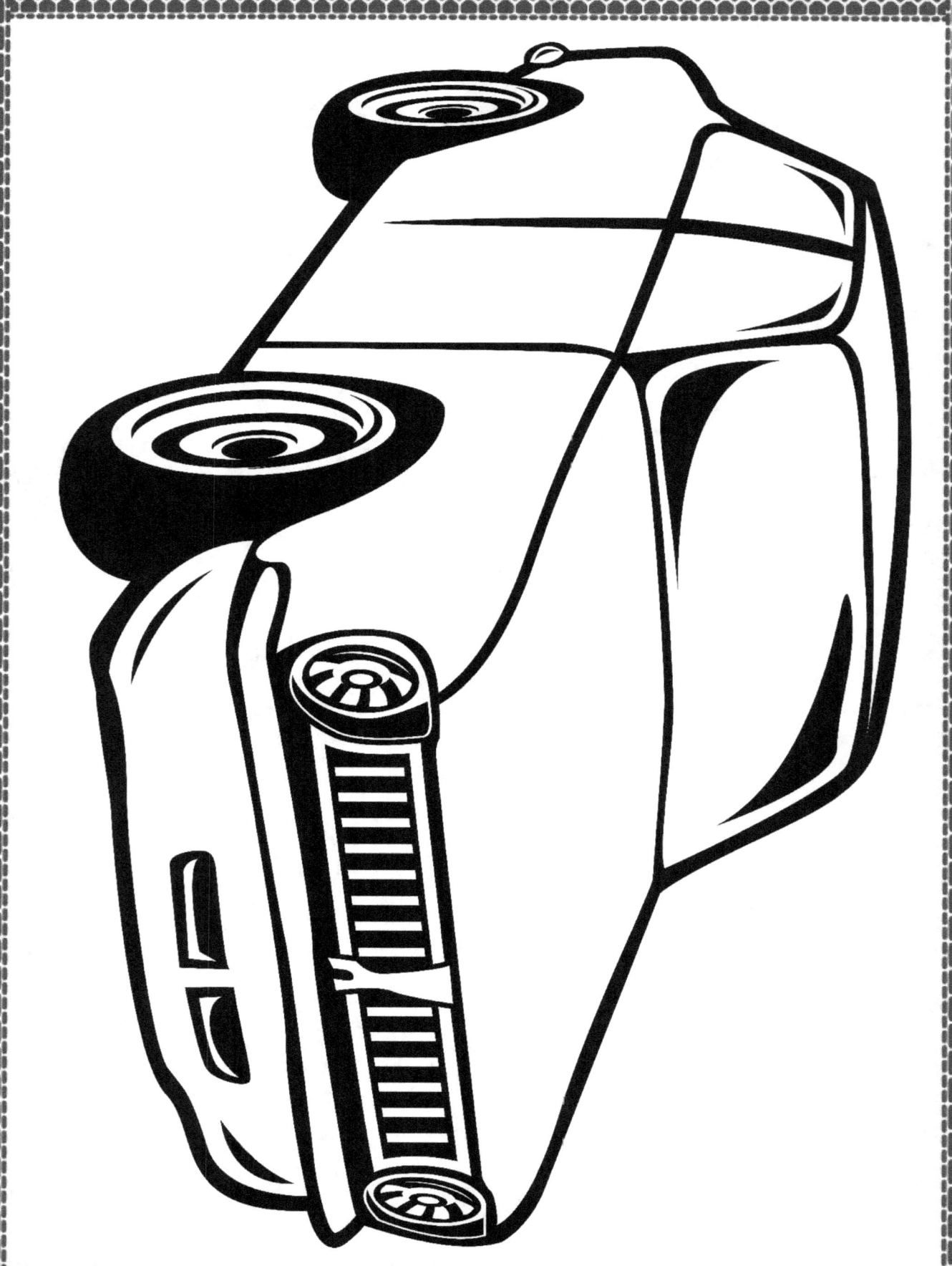

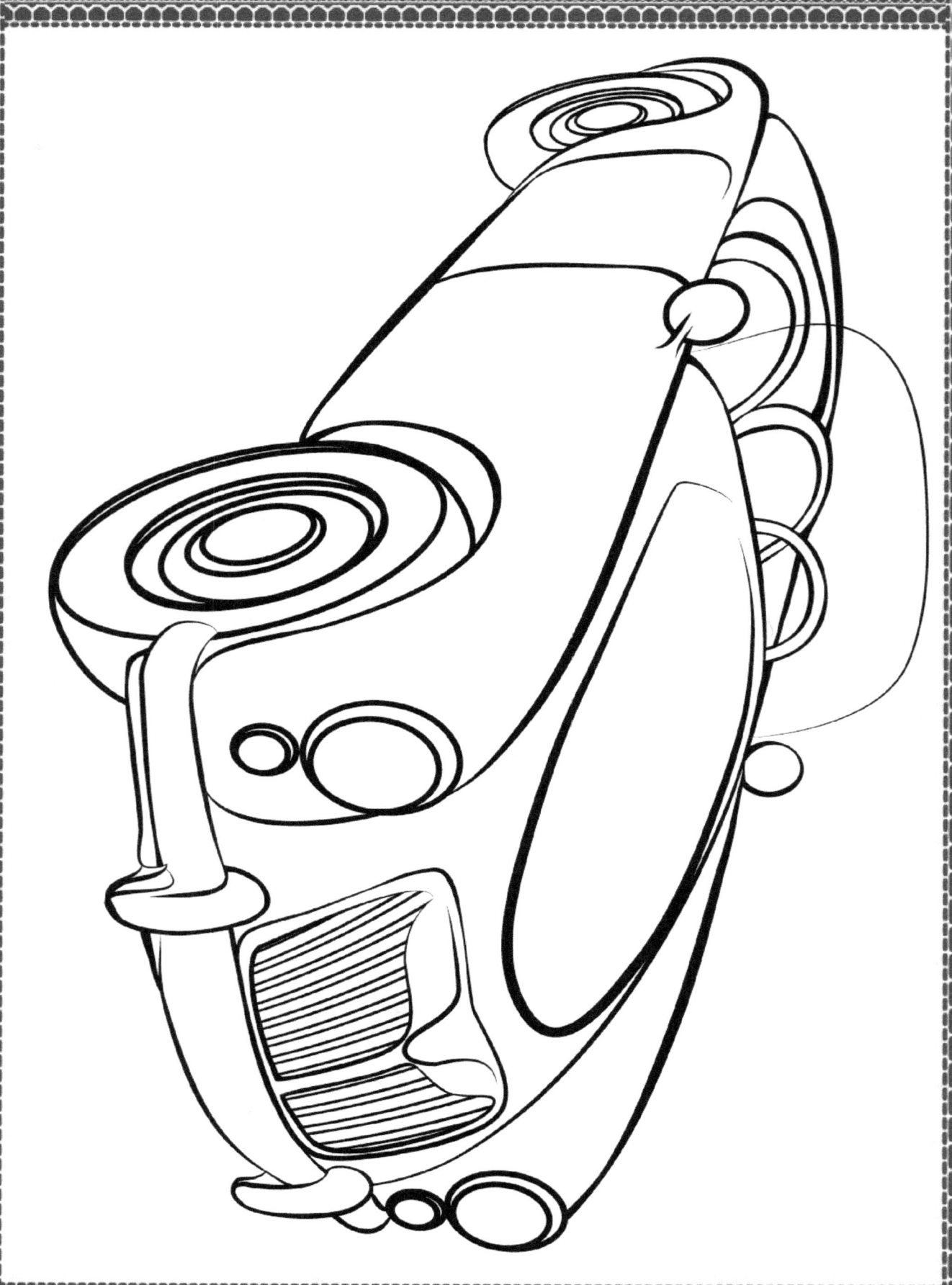

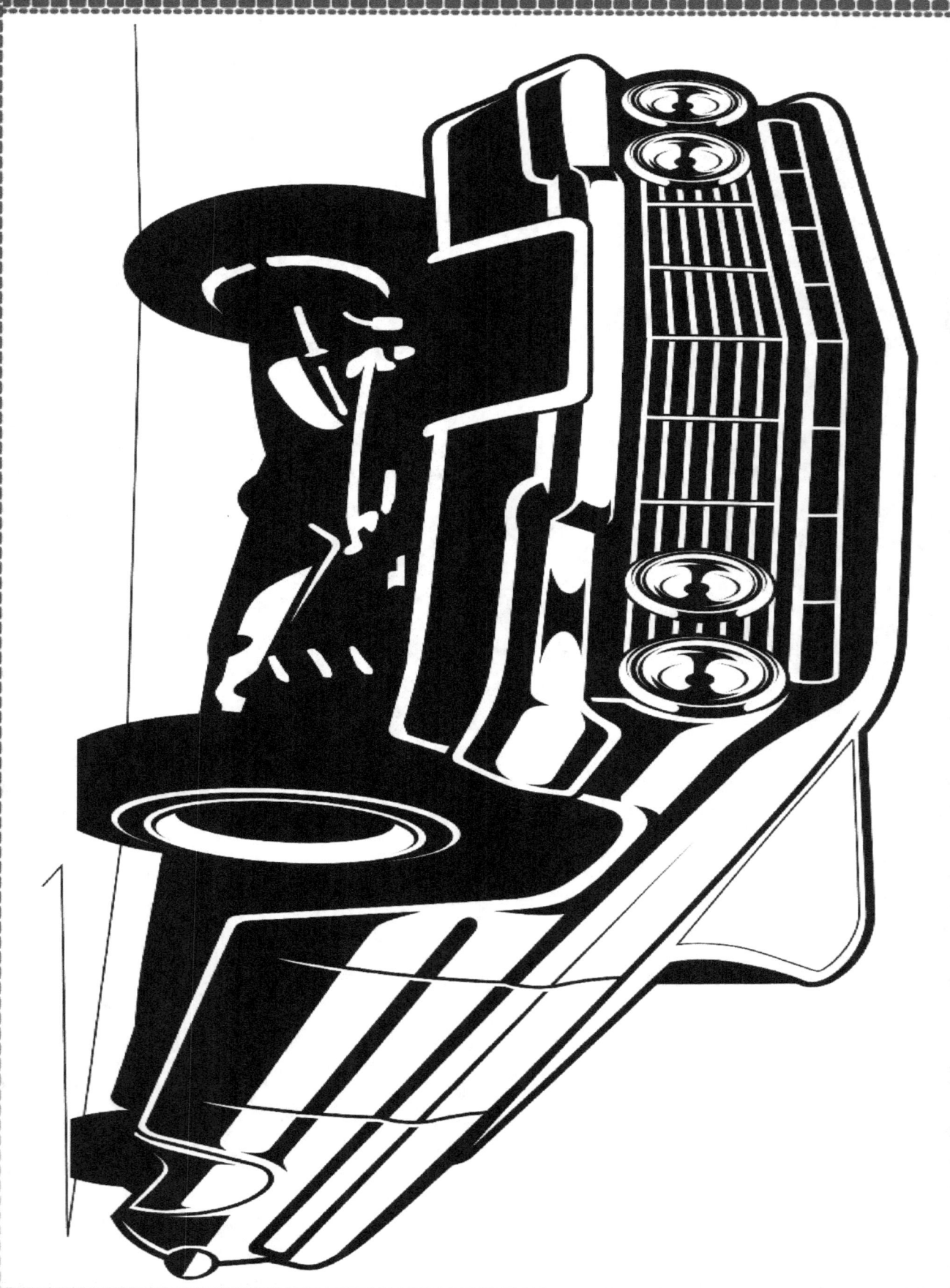

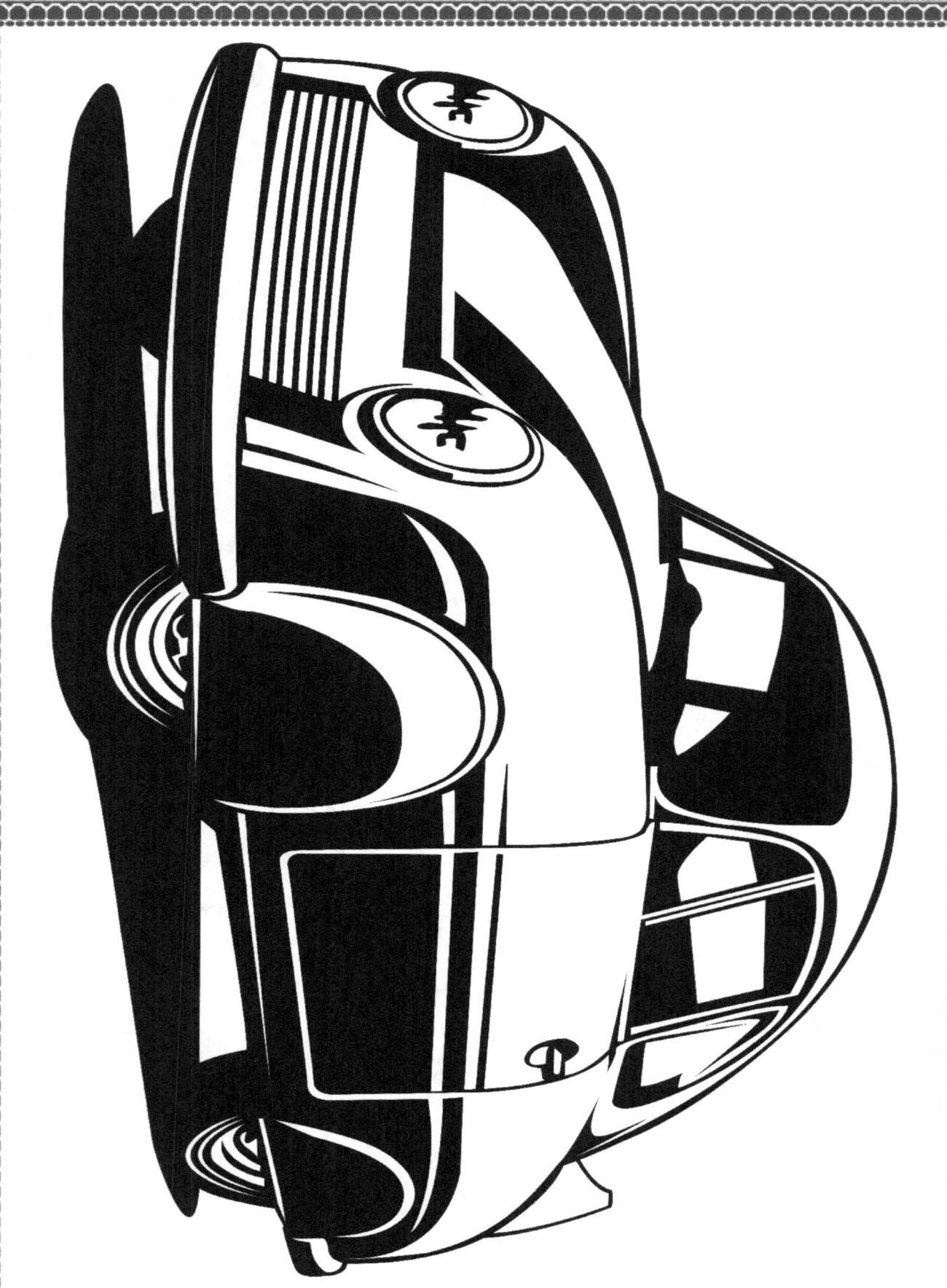

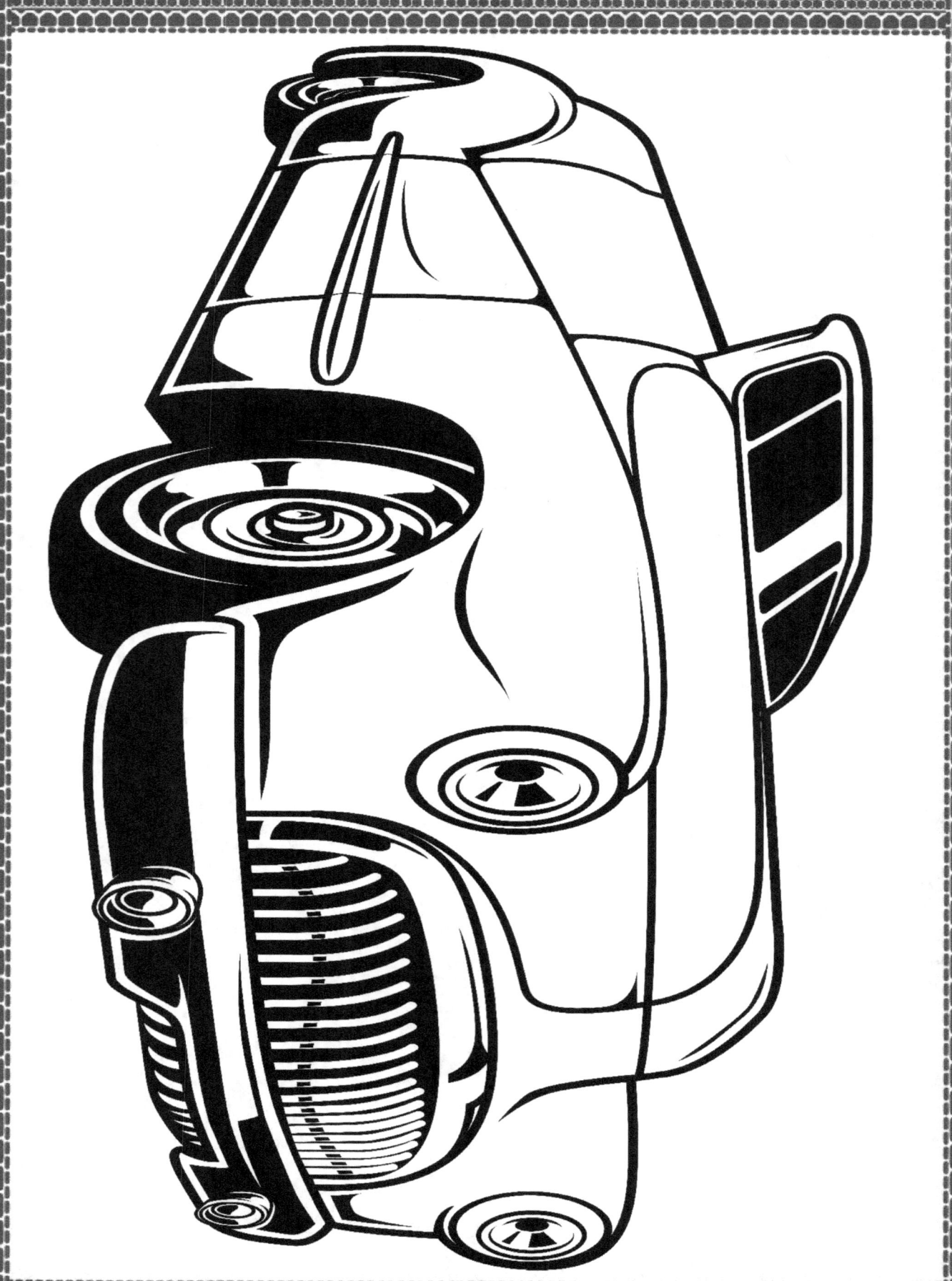

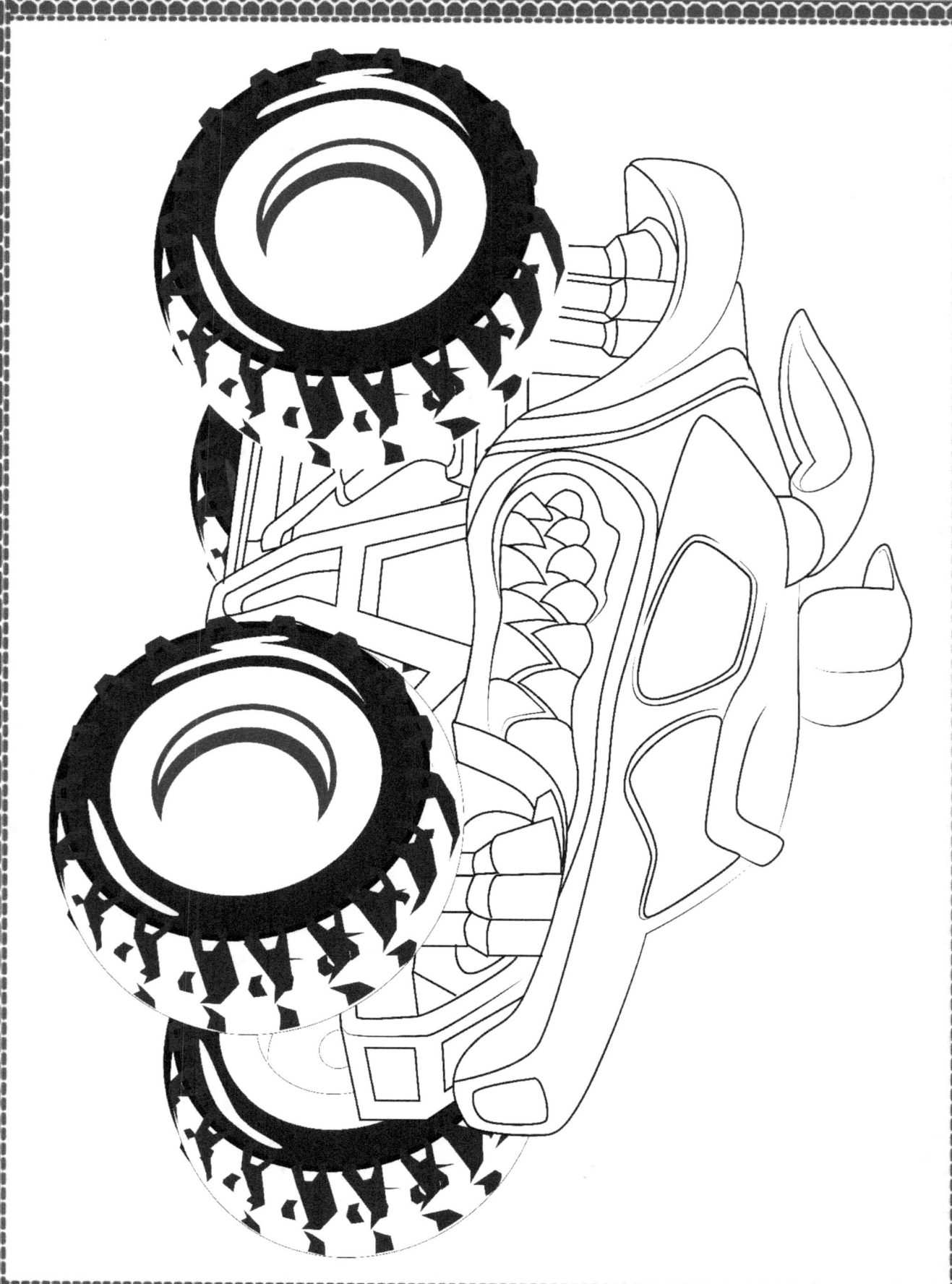

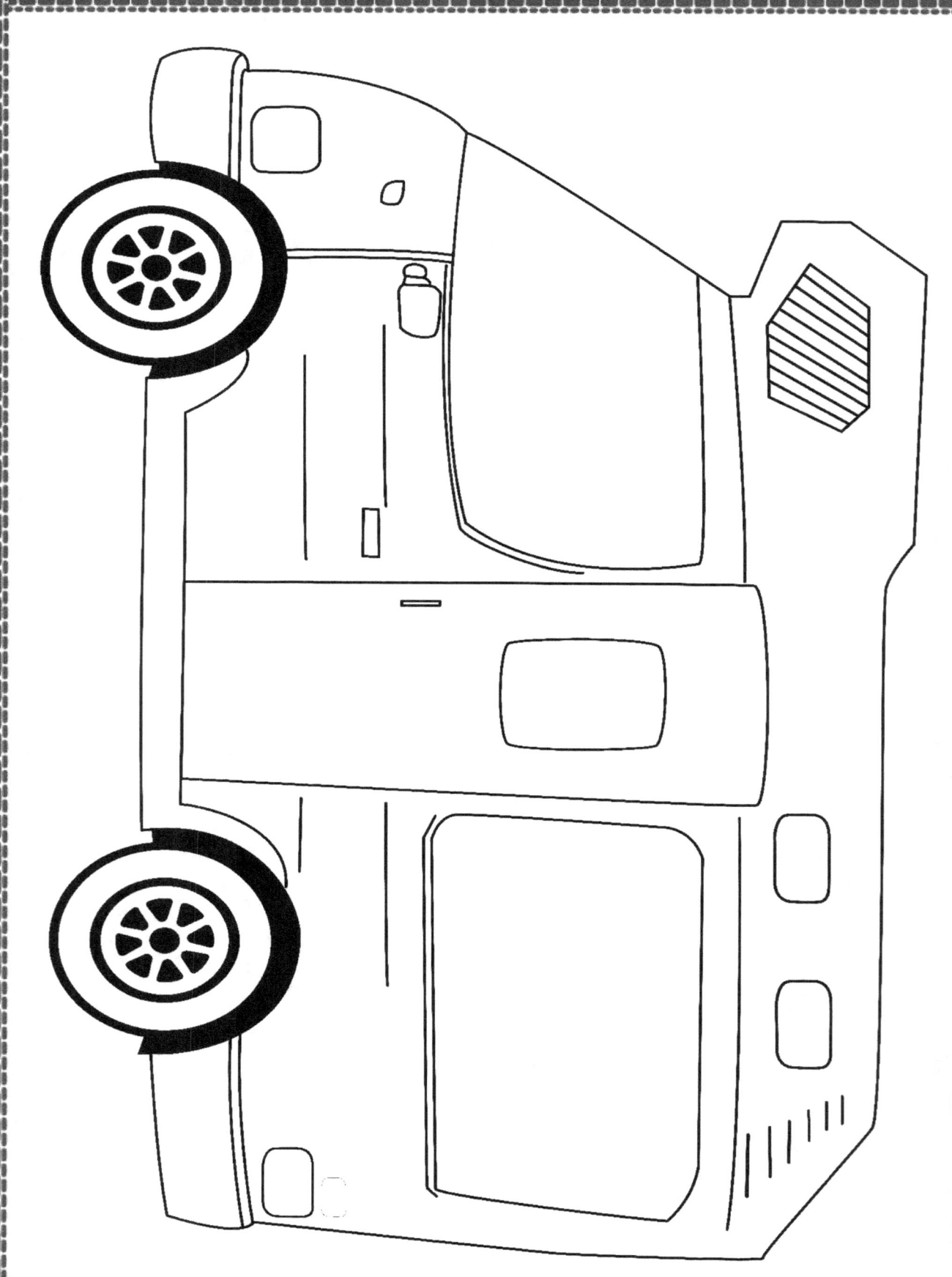

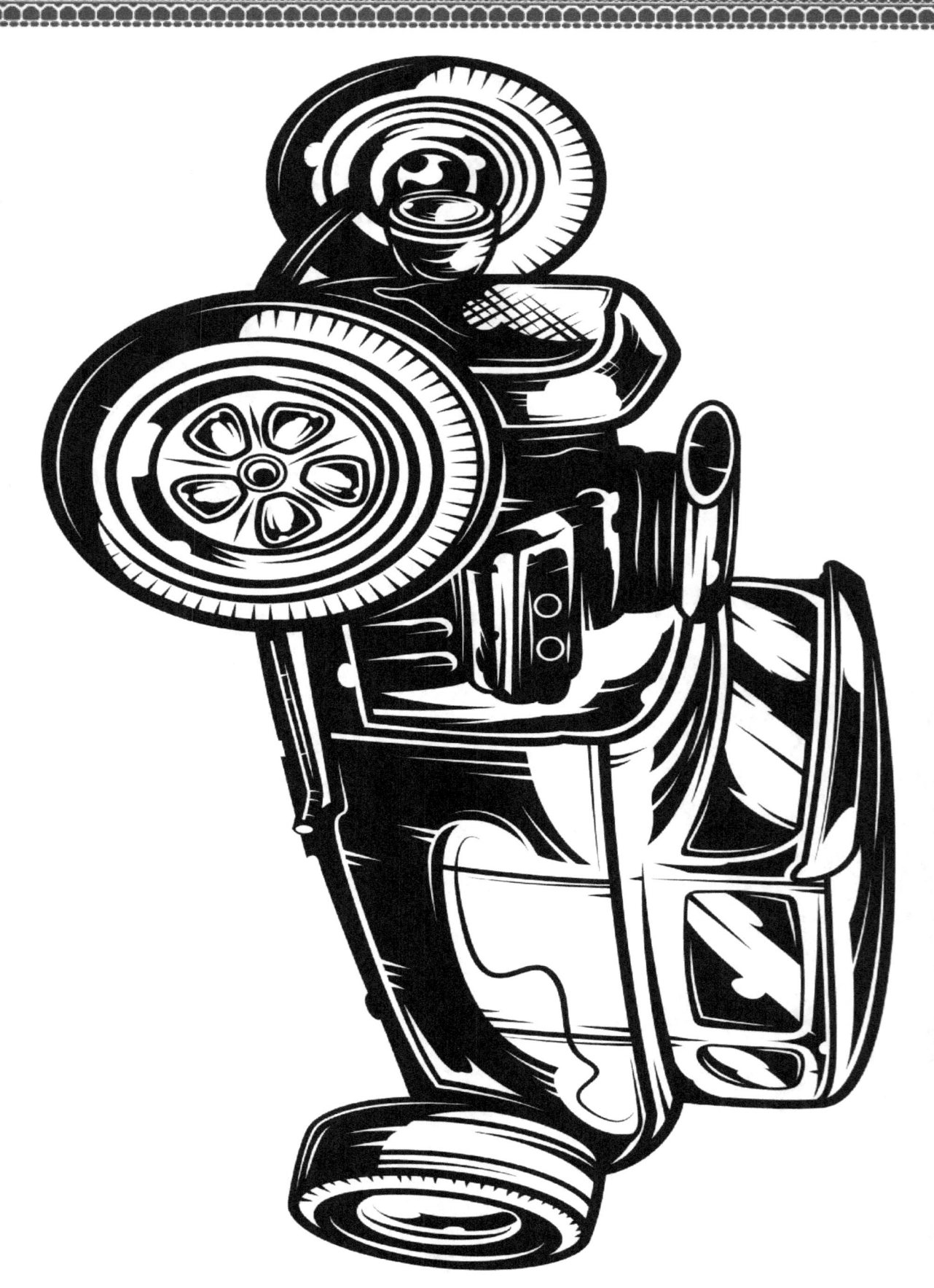

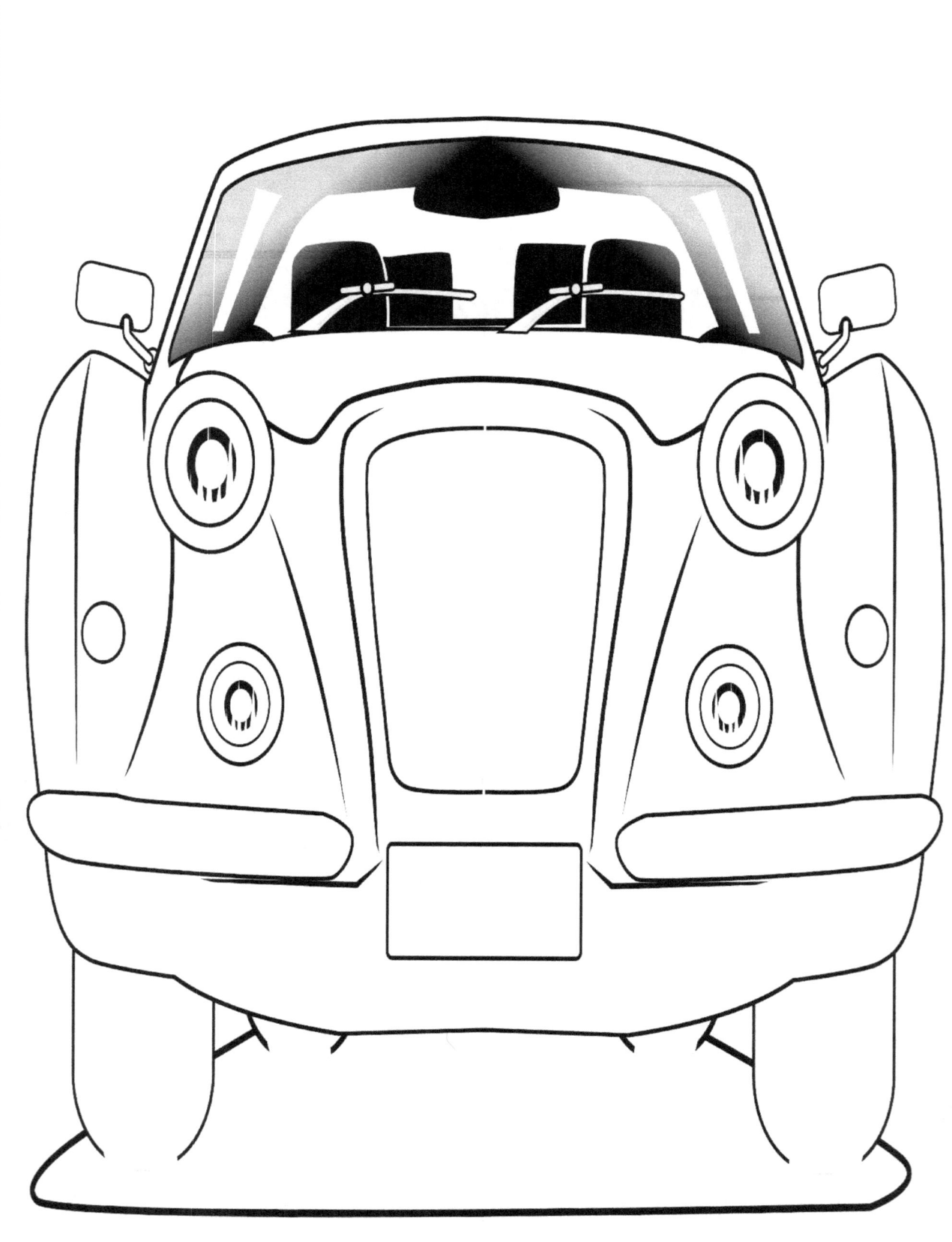

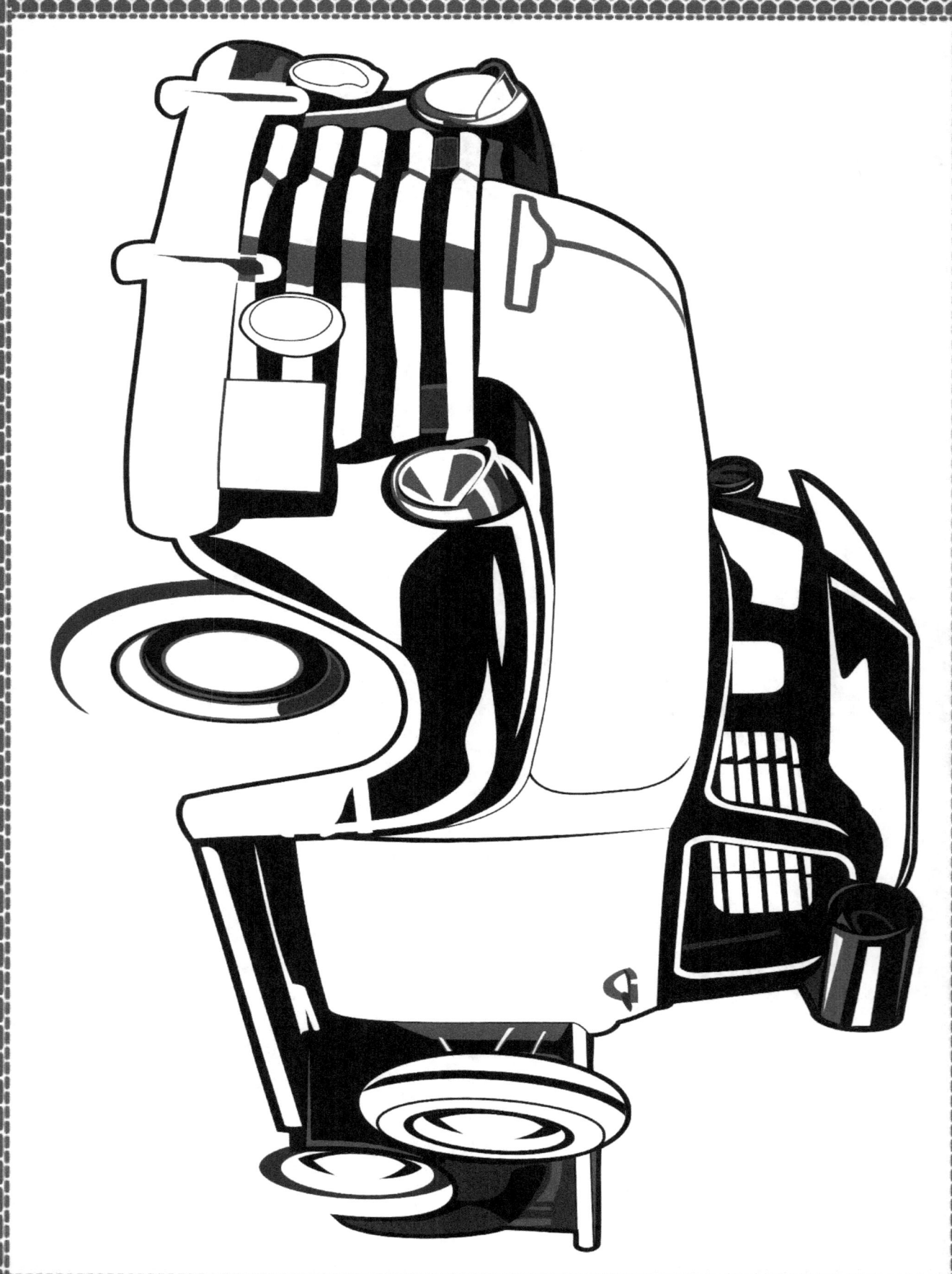

www.ingramcontent.com/pod-product-compliance
Lightning Source LLC
Chambersburg PA
CBHW080603220526
45466CB00010B/3237